BILLIARDS

BILLIARDS

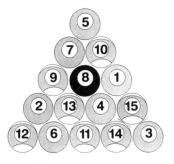

THE OFFICIAL RULES & RECORDS BOOK

Billiard Congress of America

THE LYONS PRESS
GUILFORD, CONNECTICUT
AN IMPRINT OF THE GLOBE PEQUOT PRESS

The Lyons Press is an imprint of The Globe Pequot Press.

Interior Design: Howard P. Johnson
"A Brief History of the Noble Game of Billiards" copyright © 1992 by Michael Ian Shamos.

Library of Congress Cataloging-in-Publication Data

Billiards : the official rules & records book / the Billiard Congress of America.
   p. cm.
   ISBN 1-55821-189-6
   1. Billiards. 2. Billiards—Rules. 3. Billiards—Records. I. Billiard Congress of America.

GV891.B54 1992
794.7'2—dc20   92-26888
                                                   CIP

Manufactured in the United States of America
First edition/Thirteenth printing

CONTENTS

FOREWORD

THE BILLIARD CONGRESS OF AMERICA came into existence in
1948. From its beginning, the BCA has attempted to unify our industry: bringing together players, billiard-room proprietors, retailers
and manufacturers.

Over the years, with the support of our members, the BCA has
created a wide variety of products, services and programs to contrib-
ute to the growth and participation of billiards throughout the world.

The sport of billiards has grown tremendously throughout the
years, now with over thirty-nine million participants in the United
States. Currently, more than one-third of all participants are women.
Billiards has become especially popular among families seeking a
wholesome form of recreation. There are thousands of billiard centers nationwide to accommodate the popularity of billiards. More
people play billiards or pool than jog, golf, or play tennis.

Anyone can play pool. No special strength or talent is required to
have fun playing pool. Young and old alike find the sport to be
challenging, interactive and entertaining. This book was designed to
provide both new and experienced players with consistent rules and
information on the sport of billiards. We hope through exposure to
clear and accurate rules and information, you will appreciate the
sport of billiards as do many participants worldwide.

THE BILLIARD CONGRESS OF AMERICA

A BRIEF HISTORY OF THE NOBLE GAME OF BILLIARDS

By MIKE SHAMOS

The history of billiards is long and very rich. The game has been played by kings and commoners, presidents, mental patients, ladies, gentlemen, and hustlers alike. It evolved from a lawn game similar to the croquet played sometime during the 15th century in Northern Europe and probably in France. Play was moved indoors to a wooden table with green cloth to simulate grass, and a simple border was placed around the edges. The balls were shoved, rather than struck, with wooden sticks called "maces." The term "billiard" is derived from French, either from the word "billart," one of the wooden sticks, or "bille," a ball.

The game was originally played with two balls on a six-pocket table with a hoop similar to a croquet wicket and an upright stick used as a target. All of these items can be seen in the illustration below which shows Louis XIV, the King of France, wearing a hat and

King Louis XIV playing billiards with a mace, 1694. Even for a monarch, playing by candlelight on early equipment must have been a challenge.

playing at his Court in 1694. During the eighteenth century, the hoop and target gradually disappeared, leaving only the balls and pockets. Most of our information about early billiards comes from accounts of playing by royalty and other nobles. It has been known as the "Noble Game of Billiards" since the early 1800's, but there is evidence that people from all walks of life have played the game since its inception. In 1600, the game was familiar enough to the public that Shakespeare mentioned it in *Antony and Cleopatra*. Seventy-five years later, the first book of billiard rules remarked of England that there were "few Towns of note therein which hath not a publick Billiard-Table."

The cue stick was developed in the late 1600's. When the ball lay near a rail, the mace was very inconvenient to use because of its large head. In such a case, the player would turn the mace around and use its handle to strike the ball. The handle was called a "queue"—meaning"tail"—from which we get the word "cue." For a long time only men were allowed to use the cue; women were forced to use the mace because it was felt they were more likely to rip the cloth with the sharper cue.

Tables originally had flat vertical walls for rails and their only function was to keep the balls from falling off. They resembled river banks and even used to be called "banks." Players discovered that balls could bounce off the rails and began deliberately aiming at them. Thus a "bank shot" is one in which a ball is made to rebound from a cushion as part of the shot.

Billiard equipment improved rapidly in England after 1800, largely because of the Industrial Revolution. Chalk was used to increase friction between the ball and the cue stick even before cues had tips. The leather cue tip, with which a player can apply side-spin to the ball, was perfected by 1823. Visitors from England showed Americans how to use spin which explains why it is called "English" in the United States but nowhere else. (The British themselves refer to it as "side.") The two-piece cue arrived in 1829. Slate became popular as a material for table beds around 1835. Goodyear discovered vulcanization of rubber in 1839 and by 1845 it was used to make billiard cushions. By 1850 the billiard table had essentially evolved into its current form.

The dominant billiard game in Britain from about 1770 until the 1920's was English Billiards, played with three balls and six pockets on a large rectangular table. A two-to-one ratio of length to width became standard in the 18th century. Before then, there were no fixed table dimensions. The British billiard tradition is carried on today primarily through the game of Snooker, a complex and colorful game combining offensive and defensive aspects and played on the same equipment as English Billiards but with 22 balls instead of three. The British appetite for Snooker is approached only by the American passion for baseball; it is possible to see Snooker competition every day in Britain.

BILLIARDS IN THE UNITED STATES

How billiards came to America has not been positively established. There are tales that it was brought to St. Augustine by the Spaniards in the 1580's but research has failed to reveal any trace of the game there. More likely it was brought over by Dutch and English settlers. A number of American cabinetmakers in the 1700's turned out exquisite billiard tables, although in small quantities. Nevertheless, the game did spread throughout the Colonies. Even George Washington was reported to have won a match in 1748. By 1830, despite primitive equipment, public rooms devoted entirely to billiards appeared. The most famous of them was Bassford's, a New York room that catered to stockbrokers. Here a number of American versions of billiards were developed, including Pin Pool, played with small wooden targets like miniature bowling pins, and Fifteen-Ball Pool, described later.

The American billiard industry and the incredible rise in popularity of the game are due to Michael Phelan, the father of American billiards. Phelan emigrated from Ireland and in 1850 wrote the first American book on the game. He was influential in devising rules and setting standards of behavior. An inventor, he added diamonds to the table to assist in aiming, and developed new table and cushion designs. He was also the first American billiard columnist. On January 1, 1859, the first of his weekly articles appeared in *Leslie's Illustrated Weekly*. A few months later, Phelan won a prize of $15,000 at Detroit

Michael Phelan beating John Seereiter for $15,000 at the first important prize match in the United States, Detroit, 1859.

in the first important stake match held in the United States. He was a tireless promoter of the game and created the manufacturing company of Phelan and Collender. In 1884 the company merged with its chief competitor, J. M. Brunswick & Balke, to form the Brunswick-Balke-Collender Company, which tightly controlled all aspects of the game until the 1950's. Its successor, Brunswick Billiards, is still the largest American manufacturer.

The dominant American billiard game until the 1870's was American Four-Ball Billiards, usually played on a large (11 or 12-foot), four-pocket table with four balls—two white and two red. It was a direct extension of English Billiards. Points were scored by pocketing balls, scratching the cue ball, or by making caroms on two or three balls. A "carom" is the act of hitting two object balls with the cue ball at one stroke. With so many balls, there were many different ways of scoring and it was possible to make up to 13 points on a single shot. American Four-Ball produced two offspring, both of which surpassed it in popularity by the late 1870's. One, simple caroms played with three balls on a pocketless table, is sometimes known as "Straight Rail", the forerunner of all carom games. The other popular game was American Fifteen-Ball Pool, the predecessor of modern pocket billiards. The word "pool" means a collective bet, or ante. Many non-billiard games, such as poker, involve a pool but it was to pocket billiards that the name became attached. The term "poolroom" now means a place where pool is played, but in the 19th century a poolroom was a betting parlor for horse racing. Pool tables were installed so patrons could pass the time between races. The two became connected in the public mind, but the unsavory connotation of "poolroom" came from the betting that took place there, not from billiards.

Fifteen-Ball Pool was played with 15 object balls, numbered 1 through 15. For sinking a ball, the player received a number of points equal to the value of the ball. The sum of the ball values in a rack is 120, so the first player who received more than half the total, or 61, was the winner. This game, also called "61-Pool", was used in the first American championship pool tournament held in 1878 and won by Cyrille Dion, a Canadian. In 1888, it was thought more fair to count the number of balls pocketed by a player and not their numerical value. Thus Continuous Pool replaced Fifteen-Ball Pool as the championship game. The player who sank the last ball of a rack would break the next rack and his point total would be kept "continuously" from one rack to the next.

Eight-Ball was invented shortly after 1900; Straight Pool followed in 1910. Nine-Ball seems to have developed around 1920. One-Pocket has ancestors that are older than any of these; the idea of the game was described in 1775 and complete rules for a British form appeared in 1869.

From 1878 until 1956, pool and billiard championship tournaments were held almost annually, with one-on-one challenge matches filling the remaining months. At times, including during the Civil War, billiard results received wider coverage than war news. Players were so renowned that cigarette cards were issued featuring them. The BCA Hall of Fame honors many players from this era, including Jacob Schaefer, Sr. and his son, Jake Jr., Frank Taberski, Alfredo De Oro, and Johnny Layton. The first half of this century was the era of the billiard personality. In 1906 Willie Hoppe, 18, established the world supremacy of American players by beating Maurice Vignaux of France at balkline. Balkline is a version of carom billiards with lines drawn on the table to form rectangles. When both object balls lie in the same rectangle, the number of shots that can be made is restricted. This makes the game much harder because the player must cause one of the balls to leave the rectangle, and, hopefully, return. When balkline lost its popularity during the 1930's, Hoppe began a new career in three-cushion billiards which he dominated until his retirement in 1952. Hoppe was a true American legend—a boy of humble roots whose talent was discovered early, a world champion as a teenager, and a gentleman who held professional titles for almost 50 years. One newspaper reported that under his manipulation, the balls moved "as if under a magic spell." To many fans, billiards meant Hoppe.

While the term "billiards" refers to all games played on billiard tables, with or without pockets, some people take billiards to mean carom games only and use pool for pocket games. Carom games, particularly balkline, dominated public attention until 1919, when Ralph Greenleaf's pool playing captured the nation's attention. For the next 20 years he gave up the title on only a few occasions. Through the 1930's, both pool and billiards, particularly three-cushion billiards, shared the spotlight. In 1941 the Mosconi era began and carom games declined in importance. Pool went to war several times as a popular recreation for the troops. Professional players toured military posts giving exhibitions; some even worked in the defense industry. But the game had more trouble emerging from World War II than it had getting into it. Returning soldiers were in a mood to buy houses and build careers, and the charm of an afternoon spent at the pool table was a thing of the past. Room after room closed quietly and by the end of the 1950's it looked as though the game might pass into oblivion. Willie Mosconi, who won or successfully defended the pocket billiard title 19 times, retired as champion in 1956.

Billiards was revived by two electrifying events, one in 1961, the other in 1986. The first was the release of the movie, *The Hustler,* based on the novel by Walter Tevis. The black-and-white film depicted the dark life of a pool hustler with Paul Newman in the title role. The sound of clicking balls sent America into a billiard frenzy. New rooms opened all over the country and for the remainder of the 60's pool flourished until social concerns, the Vietnam War, and a desire for outdoor coeducational activities led to a decline in billiard interest. By 1985, there were only two public rooms left in Manhattan, down from several thousand during the 1930's. In 1986, *The Color of Money,* a sequel to *The Hustler* with Paul Newman in the same role and Tom Cruise as an up-and-coming professional, brought the excitement of pool to a new generation. The result was the opening of "upscale" rooms catering to people whose senses would have been offended by the old rooms if they had ever seen them. This trend began slowly in 1987 and has since surged, even resulting in a public stock offering in 1991 by Jillian's, a Boston-based room chain.

While the game has had its heroes since the early 1800's, it has had to wage a constant battle for respectability. Poolrooms were often the target of politicians and legislators eager to show an ability to purge immorality from the community. Even today, obtaining a billiard license can require compliance with antiquated regulations. In the 1920's, the poolroom was an environment in which men gathered to loiter, smoke, fight, bet, and play. The rooms of the 1990's bear no resemblance to those of earlier times. The new rooms have a cachet approaching that of chic restaurants and night clubs. They offer quality equipment, expert instruction, and the chance for people to meet socially for a friendly evening. Being totally without stigma, these rooms are responsible for introducing an entire new audience to the game and are resulting in the greatest surge in billiard interest in the United States in over a century.

WOMEN IN BILLIARDS

Until very recently, billiards was completely dominated by men. The atmosphere of the poolroom was very forbidding and a woman would have had trouble being accepted there. Nonetheless, women have been enthusiastic players since the game was brought up from the

"The Billiard Room of the Grand Union Hotel, Saratoga, New York", 1875. Pool rooms were overwhelmingly male until almost 1900.

"An Evening at Billiards", 1896. At home and in private clubs, women have been playing billiards for hundreds of years.

ground in the 15th century. For over two hundred years women of fashion have played. Since the 1890's, there has always been at least one prominent female professional on the scene, from May Kaarlus, a spectacular turn-of-the-century trick-shot artist, to Ruth McGinnis, who toured with Willie Mosconi in the 1930's and could beat most men, to Dorothy Wise, winner of the first five U.S. Open tournaments for women, and Jean Balukas, who took the next seven. Today there are enough women professionals to merit a separate organization, the WPBA, to solicit commercial sponsorship and organize tournaments. It is very difficult for a woman to develop billiard skill because male players, her family, and friends usually do not support her efforts and it is not easy to find experienced women instructors or coaches. As this situation changes, we can expect women to equal men in ability and take the game to even greater heights.

—Mike Shamos is Curator of The Billiard Archive, a non-profit organization set up to preserve the game's history.

BCA EQUIPMENT SPECIFICATIONS

TABLE SIZES (IN FEET).

Pocket billiard tables .... 4 by 8 and 4½ by 9
Carom billiard tables .... 4½ by 9 and 5 by 10
American snooker tables .... 4½ by 9 and 5 by 10

PLAYING AREA.

Measured from the cloth-covered nose of cushion rubber to the opposite cushion rubber, both width and length:

4 by 8 table .... playing area of 44″ width by 88″ length
4 by 8 table .... playing area of 46″ width by 92″ length
4½ by 9 table .... playing area of 50″ width by 100″ length
5 by 10 table .... playing area of 56″ width by 112″ length
BCA will sanction tournament play on home and coin-operated tables, produced in sizes other than those recognized above, if the playing area width is one-half the length, measured cushion to opposite cushion.

TABLE—BED HEIGHT.

The table-bed playing surface, when measured from the bottom of the table leg, will be 29¼″ (plus or minus ¼″) in height.

POCKET OPENINGS.

Pocket-billiard tables: Pocket openings are measured between opposing cushion noses at the points where the nose changes direction into the pocket throat.

Corner .... 4⅞″ minimum to 5⅛″ maximum
Side .... 5⅜″ minimum to 5⅝″ maximum
Vertical pocket angle .... 12° ± 1°
Snooker tables: Pocket openings are measured between the opposing cushion noses at the point where the nose meets the slate opening in the pocket throat.

Corner .... 3⅜″ minimum to 3⅝″ maximum
Side .... 4¹⁄₁₆″ minimum to 4⁵⁄₁₆″ maximum

PLAYING BED.

The playing surface must be capable, either by its own strength or a combination of its strength and that of the table frame, of maintaining an overall flatness within ±.020" lengthwise and .010" across the width. Further, this surface should have an additional deflection not to exceed .030" when loaded with a concentrated static force of 200 pounds at its center. If more than one slab is employed, the slab joints must be in the same plane within .005" after leveling and shimming. The bed must be covered with a billiard fabric, the major portion of which is made of wool, with proper tension to avoid unwanted rolling of the ball. Commercial tables must have a 1" 3-piece set of slate with a wooden frame minimum ¾" attached to slate. All playing surfaces must be secured to the frame with screws or bolts.

CUSHIONS.

Rubber cushions should be triangular in shape and molded with the conventional K-66 profile with a base of 1³⁄₁₆" and a nose height of 1", with control fabric molded to the top and base area of the cushion. On carom-billiard tables, the triangular K-55 profile cushion is to be maintained, with the control fabric on the underside of the cushion to affect a slower rebound action. On snooker tables, the triangular K-66 profile or L-shaped snooker cushion is to be used. The balance of the rail section to which the rubber cushion is glued should be of hardwood construction and attached to the slate bed with a minimum of three heavy-duty, threaded rail bolts per rail.

BILLIARD BALLS.

Molded and finished in a perfect shape, with both dynamic and static balance, in the following weights and diameters as used in the following games:

Pocket-billiard balls
    Weight: 5½ to 6 oz. . . . . *Diameter: 2¼"
Carom-billiard balls
    Weight: 7 to 7½ oz. . . . . *Diameter: 2²⁷⁄₆₄"
                                                                                                    2³⁄₈"
                                                                                                    2⁷⁄₁₆"

Snooker balls
    Weight: 5 to 5½ oz. . . . . *Diameter 2⅛"
                                                                                                    2¹⁄₁₆"
*Diameter tolerance of (plus or minus) .005".

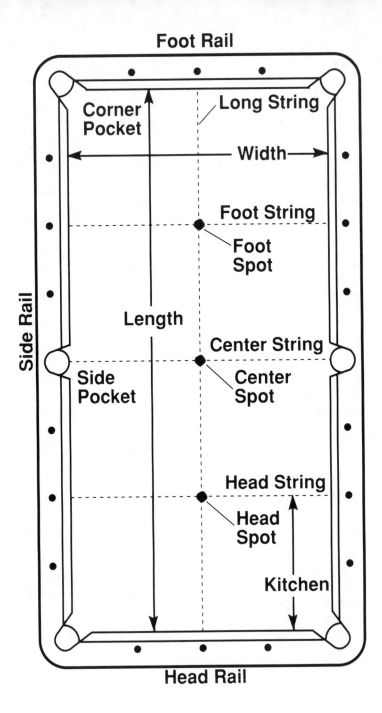

FIGURE 3–1

GLOSSARY OF BILLIARD TERMS

The following glossary contains billiard terms and definitions essential to the game rules provided in this book. In addition to definitions, there are also many references to equipment, accessories and phrases commonly used by billiard players.

Each definition begins with the term in boldface type, followed by a parenthetical notation of the game variation or classification in which the term is used, or to which it primarily applies.

Where a figure or other supplemental information is available elsewhere in this book, it is referenced parenthetically following the definition.

Angled. (Snooker, pocket games) When the corner of a pocket prevents a player from shooting the cue ball directly at an object ball. (See *corner hooked.*)

Angle shot. (Pocket games) A shot that requires the cue ball to drive the object ball other than straight ahead. (See *cut shot.*)

Apex of triangle. (Pocket games) The position in the grouping of object balls that is on the foot spot; the front ball position of the pyramid or rack.

Around the table. (Carom games) Describes shots in which the cue ball contacts three or more cushions, usually including the two short cushions, in an effort to score.

Balance point. (General) The point on a cue at which it would remain level if held by a single support, usually about eighteen inches from the butt end.

Ball in hand. (Pocket games) See *cue ball in hand.*

Ball on. (Snooker) A colored (non-red) ball a player intends to legally pocket; same as on ball.

Balk. (Snooker) The intervening space between the bottom cushion and the balkline.

Balkline. (Snooker) A straight line drawn twenty-nine inches from the face of the bottom cushion and parallel to it.

Bank shot. (Pocket games) A shot in which the object ball is driven to one or more cushions before it is pocketed; incidental contact as a ball moves along and adjacent to a cushion does not qualify as a cushion or bank. It is not an obvious shot and must be called in games requiring called shots. (See *kick shot*.)

Bed of table. (General) The flat, cloth-covered surface of the table within the cushions; the playing area exclusive of the cushions.

Billiard. (Carom games) A count or score; a successful shot.

Blind draw. (General) A method used to determine pairings or bracketing of players in tournaments that assures random placement or pairing of contestants.

Bottle. (Pocket games) A specially shaped leather or plastic container used in various games; also called the shake bottle.

Bottom cushion. (Snooker) The cushion located at the head of a snooker table, closest to the D.

Break. (Pocket games) See *open break* and *opening-break shot*.

Break. (Snooker) Total scored in one inning.

Breaking violation. (Pocket games) A violation of special rules which apply only to the opening-break shot of certain games. Unless specified in individual game rules, a breaking violation is not a foul.

Bridge. (General) The hand configuration that holds and guides the shaft of the cue during play (See *mechanical bridge*.)

Burst. (Forty-one pocket billiards) Scoring a total of more than forty-one points.

Butt of cue. (General) The larger end of a cue, opposite the tip. On a two-piece cue, the butt extends up to the joint.

Call shot. (Pocket games) Requirement that a player designate, in advance of each shot, the ball to be made and the pocket into which it will be made. In calling the shot, it is never necessary to indicate details such as the number of cushions, banks, kisses, caroms, etc.

Called ball. (Pocket games) The ball the player has designated to be pocketed.

Called pocket. (Pocket games) The pocket into which a player has designated a ball to be made.

Carom. (General) To bounce off or glance off an object ball or cushion; a shot in which the cue ball bounces off one ball into another.

Carom, Scoring. (General) Contact by the cue ball with object balls, the bottle or cushions in such a way that a legal score is made, according to specific game rules.

Center Spot. (General) The center point of a table's playing surface.

Chalk. (General) A dry, slightly abrasive substance that is applied to the cue tip to help assure a nonslip contact between the cue tip and the cue ball.

Chuck nurse. (Straight rail billiards) A scoring technique used when one object ball rests against the cushion and the second object ball is to one side of the first ball and away from the cushion. Cue ball strikes the object ball at the cushion so that the cue ball just comes back to touch (carom) the second object ball without moving it out of position for a similar subsequent shot.

Clean bank. (Bank pocket billiards) A shot in which the object ball being played does not touch any other object balls (i.e., no kisses, no combinations).

Clear ball. (Carom games) The all-white ball, devoid of any markings, used in carom games (See *spot ball.*)

Combination. (Pocket games) Shot in which the cue ball first strikes a ball other than the one to be pocketed, with the ball initially contacted in turn striking one or more other balls in an effort to score.

Combination on. (Pocket games) Two or more balls positioned in such a way that a ball can be driven into a called pocket with a combination shot; often called a dead combo or an on combo.

Combination on. (Snooker) See *plant.*

Contact point. (General) The precise point of contact between the cue ball and the object ball when the cue ball strikes the object ball. (See chapter 4.)

Corner hooked. (Pocket games, Snooker) When the corner of a pocket prevents shooting the cue ball in a straight path directly at an object ball, the cue ball is corner hooked; same as angled.

Count. (General) A score; a successful shot.

Count, The. (General) The running score at any point during a player's inning in games where numerous points are scored successively.

Cross corner. (Pocket games) Term used to describe a bank shot that will rebound from a cushion and into a corner pocket.

Cross side. (Pocket games) Term used to describe a bank shot that will rebound from a cushion into a side pocket.

Cross table shot. (Carom games) Shot in which scoring is accomplished by driving the cue ball across the table between the long cushions.

Crotch. (Carom games) The corner area of a carom table. The four crotches are defined as those spaces within crotch lines drawn between points on the side and end cushions 4½ inches from the corners of the playing surface to the cushions.

Crutch. (General) Slang term for the mechanical bridge.

Cue. (General) Tapered device, usually wooden, used to strike the cue ball to execute carom- or pocket-billiard shots. Also called cue stick.

Cue ball. (General) The white, unnumbered ball that is always struck by the cue during play.

Cue ball in hand. (Pocket games) Cue ball may be put into play anywhere on the playing surface.

Cue ball in hand behind the head string. (Pocket games) Cue ball may be put into play anywhere between the head string and the cushion on the head end of the table not in contact with an object ball. (See Figure 3-1.)

Cue ball in hand within the D. (Snooker) The cue ball is in hand within the D when it has entered a pocket or has been forced off the table. The base of the cue ball may be placed anywhere within or on the D. It remains in hand until the player strikes the cue ball with the tip of the cue or a foul is committed while the ball is on the table.

Cue tip. (General) A piece of specially processed leather attached to the shaft end of the cue that contacts the cue ball when a shot is executed.

Cushion. (General) The cloth-covered rubber which borders the inside of the rails on carom- and pocket-billiard tables; together the cushions form the outer perimeter of the basic playing surface.

Cut shot. (Pocket games) A shot in which the cue ball contacts the object ball to one side or the other of full center, thus driving it in a direction other than that of the initial cue-ball path. (See chapter 4.)

D. (Snooker) An area, semicircular in shape, with the straight side formed by the head string and the semicircle being described by an arc drawn with the head spot as the center point. The radius of the semicircle is determined by the size of the table being used. (See Figure 10-1.)

Dead ball. (Pocket games) A cue ball stroked in such a manner that virtually all of the speed and/or spin of the cue ball is transferred to the object ball, the cue ball retaining very little or none after contact.

Dead-ball shot. (Pocket games) A shot in which a dead-ball stroke is employed; often called a kill shot, because of the relative lack of cue-ball motion after contact with the object ball.

Dead combination. (Pocket games) See *combination on.*

Diamonds. (General) Inlays or markings on the table rails that are used as reference or target points. Though used in pocket games, the diamonds are essential for the utilization of numerous mathematical systems employed by carom-games players. (See chapter 13.)

Draw shot. (General) A shot in which the cue ball is struck below center with an effective stroke, resulting in the cue ball reversing direction after contact with the object ball, because of the underspin applied to the cue ball.

Drop pockets. (Pocket games) Type of pockets with no automatic return of the balls to the foot end of the table; balls must be removed manually.

Double-draw shot. (General) A shot in which such extreme and effective draw stroke is employed that when the cue ball reverses direction after contact with the object ball into a cushion and rebounds, the underspin (draw) overcomes the direction and speed of the rebound, causing the cue ball to stop and reverse direction again.

Double elimination. (General) A tournament format in which a player is not eliminated until he has sustained two match losses.

Double hit. (General) A shot in which the cue ball is struck twice by the cue tip on the same stroke. (See chapters 7 and 12.)

Double round-robin. (General) A tournament format in which each contestant in a field plays each of the other players twice.

English. (General) Side spin applied to the cue ball by striking it off center; used to alter the natural roll of the cue ball and/or the object ball.

Feather shot. (General) A shot in which the cue ball barely touches or grazes the object ball; an extremely thin cut.

Ferrule. (General) A piece of protective material (usually white ivory or plastic) at the end of the cue shaft, on which the cue tip is attached.

Follow shot. (General) A shot in which the cue ball is struck above center, resulting in the cue ball continuing in the same general direction of the stroke with the object ball. Because of the overspin applied to the cue ball, the speed of the cue ball will be faster than that of natural roll.

Follow-through. (General) The movement of the cue after contact with the cue ball through the area previously occupied by the cue ball. (See chapter 4.)

Foot of table. (General) The end of a carom or pocket-billiard table at which the balls are racked or positioned at the start of a game.

Foot spot. (General) The point on the foot end of the table where imaginary lines drawn between the center diamonds of the short rails and the second diamonds of the long rails intersect. (See Figure 3-1.)

Foot string. (General) A line on the foot end of the table between the second diamonds of the long rails, passing through the foot spot. (See Figure 3-1.)

Force. (General) The inertia or power applied on the stroke to the cue ball, which may result in distortion and altering of natural angles and action of the ball.

Force draw. (General) Extreme underspin applied to the cue ball. Usually refers to shots in which the cue ball travels in the direction of the stroke for a distance before the underspin takes effect: the cue ball stops and then draws back in direction.

Force follow. (General) An extreme follow shot, with the term generally used in reference to shots in which the cue ball is shot directly at and then "through" an object ball, with a pronounced hesitation or stop before the overspin propels the cue ball forward in the general direction of the stroke.

Foul. (General) An infraction of the rules of play, as defined in either the general or the specific game rules. (Not all rule infractions are fouls). Fouls result in a penalty, also dependent on specific game rules.

Foul stroke. (General) A stroke on which a foul takes place.

Frame. The equivalent of one game in snooker.

Free ball. (Snooker) If the cue ball is snookered after a foul, the referee shall state "Free Ball." If the nonoffending player takes the next stroke he may nominate any ball as on, and for this stroke, such ball shall be regarded as, and acquire the value of, the ball on. (See chapter 10.)

Free break. (Pocket games) An opening break shot in which a wide spread of the object balls may be achieved without penalty or risk. Free breaks are detailed in individual game rules.

Frozen. (General) A ball touching another ball or cushion.

Full ball. (General) Contact of the cue ball with an object ball at a contact point on a line bisecting the centers of the cue ball and object ball. (See chapter 4.)

Game. (General) The course of play that starts when the referee has finished racking the balls, and ends at the conclusion of a legal shot which pockets the last required ball.

Game ball. (General) The ball which, if pocketed legally, would produce victory in a game.

Gather shot. (Carom games) A shot in which appropriate technique and speed is employed to drive one or more balls away from the other(s) in such a manner that when the stroke is complete, the balls have come back together closely enough to present a comparatively easy scoring opportunity for the next shot.

Grip. (General) The manner in which the butt of the cue is held in the hand. (See chapter 4.)

Gully table. (Pocket games) A table with pockets and a return system that delivers the balls as they are pocketed to a collection bin on the foot end of the table.

Handicapping. (General) Modifications in the scoring and/or rules of games to enable players of differing abilities to compete on more even terms.

Head of table. (General) The end of a carom- or pocket-billiard table from which the opening break is performed; the end normally marked with the manufacturer's nameplate.

Head spot. (General) The point on the head of the table where imaginary lines drawn between the center diamonds of the short rails and the second diamonds of the long rails intersect. (See Figure 3-1.)

Head string. (General) A line on the head end of the table between the second diamonds of the long rails, passing through the head spot. (See Diagram #1, Pg. 10.)

Hickey. (Snooker golf) Any foul.

High run. (14.1 continuous) During a specified segment of play, the greatest number of balls scored in one turn (inning) at the table.

Hold. (General) English which stops the cue ball from continuing the course of natural roll it would take after having been driven in a certain direction.

In hand. (Pocket games) See *cue ball in hand.*

In hand behind the head string. (Pocket games) See *cue ball in hand behind the head string.*

Inning. (General) A turn at the table by a player.

In-off. (Snooker) A losing hazard; that is, when the cue ball enters a pocket. The snooker equivalent of a scratch.

In the rack. (Pocket games) A ball that would interfere with the reracking of the object balls in games that extend past one rack.

Jaw. (Pocket games) The slanted part of the cushion that is cut at an angle to form the opening from the bed of the table into the pocket.

Jawed ball. (Pocket games) Generally refers to a ball that fails to drop after bouncing back and forth against the jaws of a pocket.

Joint. (General) On two-piece cues, the screw-and-thread device, approximately midway in the cue, that permits it to be broken down into two separate sections.

Jumped ball. (General) A ball that has left and remained off of the playing surface as a result of a stroke. Also, a ball that is stroked in a manner which causes it to jump over another ball.

Jump shot. (General) A shot in which the cue ball and/or an object ball rises off the bed of the table.

Key ball. (14.1 continuous) The fourteenth ball of each rack; called the key ball because it is so critical in obtaining position for the all-important first (or break) shot of each rerack of the balls.

Kick shot. (General) A shot in which the cue ball banks off a cushion(s) prior to making contact with an object ball or scoring.

Kill shot. (Pocket games) See *dead ball shot.*

Kiss. (General) Contact between balls. (See *kiss shot.*)

Kiss-out. (General) Contact, accidental or not, between balls that causes a shot to fail.

Kiss shot. (Pocket games) A shot in which more than one contact with object balls is made by the cue ball; for example, the cue ball might kiss from one object ball into another to score the latter ball. Also shots in which object balls carom off one or more other object balls to be pocketed. (Also called carom shots.)

Kitchen. (Pocket games) A slang term used to describe the area of the table between the head string and the cushion on the head end of the table. Also called the area behind the head string.

Lag. (Carom games) A shot in which the cue ball is shot off three or more cushions before contacting the object balls.

Lag for break. (General) Procedure used to determine starting player of game. Each player shoots a ball from behind the head string to the foot cushion, attempting to return the ball as closely as possible to the head cushion. (See chapters 4 and 12.)

Leave. (Pocket games) The position of the balls after a player's shot.

Long. (General) Usually refers to a ball which, due to English and stroke, travels a path with wider angles than those that are standard for such a ball if struck with natural English and moderate speed.

Long string. (Pocket games) A line drawn from the center of the foot cushion to the foot spot, and beyond if necessary, on which balls are spotted.

Losing hazard. (Snooker) Occurs when the cue ball is pocketed after contact with an object ball.

Lot. (General) Procedures used, not involving billiard skills, to determine starting player or order of play in casual or nontournament play. Common methods used are flipping coins, drawing straws, drawing cards, or drawing peas or pills.

Masse shot. (General) A shot in which extreme English is applied to the cue ball by means of elevating the cue butt at an angle to the bed of the table anywhere between 30 and 90 degrees.

Match. (General) The course of play starting when the players are ready to lag and ending after the deciding game.

Mechanical bridge. (General) A grooved device mounted on a handle, providing support for the shaft of the cue during shots difficult to reach with normal bridge hand. Also called a crutch or rake.

Miscue. (General) A stroke which results in faulty contact between the cue tip and the cue ball. Usually the cue tip slides off the cue ball without full transmission of the desired stroke.

Miss. (General) Failure to execute a completed shot.

Natural. (Carom games) A shot with only natural angle and stroke required for successful execution; a simple or easily visualized, and accomplished, scoring opportunity.

Natural English. (General) Moderate sidespin applied to the cue ball that favors the direction of the cue-ball path, giving the cue ball a natural roll and a bit more speed than a center hit.

Natural roll. (General) Movement of the cue ball with no English applied.

Nip draw. (General) A short, sharp stroke, employed when a normal draw stroke would result in a foul by drawing the cue ball back into the cue tip.

Nurses. (Carom games) Techniques whereby the balls are kept close to the cushions and each other, creating a succession of relatively easy scoring opportunities.

Object ball, The (Pocket games) The particular object ball being played on a shot.

Object balls. (General) The balls other than the cue ball on a shot.

On ball. (Snooker) See *ball on*.

Open break. (Pocket games) The requirement in certain games that a player must drive a minimum of four object balls out of the rack to the cushions in order for the shot to be legal.

Opening break shot. (General) The first shot of a game.

Peas. (Pocket games) Small plastic balls numbered one through fifteen or sixteen, use defined in specific game rules. Also called pills.

Pills. (Pocket games) See *Peas*.

Plant. (Snooker) A position of two or more red balls that allows a ball to be driven into a pocket with a combination shot.

Position. (General) The placement of the cue ball on each shot relative to the next planned shot.

Pot. (Snooker) The pocketing of an object ball.

Powder. (General) Talc or other fine, powdery substance used to facilitate free, easy movement of the cue shaft through the bridge.

Power-draw shot. (General) Extreme draw applied to the cue ball. (See *force draw*.)

Push shot. (General) A shot in which the cue tip maintains contact with the cue ball beyond the split second allowed for a normal and legally stroked shot.

Pyramid. (Pocket games) Positioning of the object balls in a triangular grouping (with the front apex ball on the foot spot), used to begin many pocket billiard games.

Pyramid spot. (Snooker) The same as the pink spot. The spot is marked midway between the center spot and the face of the top cushion.

Race. (General) Predetermined number of games necessary to win a match or set of games.

Rack. (General) The triangular equipment used for gathering the balls into the formation required by the game being played.

Rails. (General) The top surface of the table, not covered by cloth, from which the cushions protrude toward the playing surface. The head and foot rails are the short rails on those ends of the table; the right and left rails are the long rails, dictated by standing at the head end of the table and facing the foot end.

Red ball. (Carom games) The red-colored object ball. Also the name of a particular 3-cushion billiard game.

Rest. (Snooker) The mechanical bridge.

Reverse English. (General) Sidespin applied to the cue ball, that favors the opposite direction of the natural cue-ball path, which causes it to rebound from an object ball or a cushion at a slower speed than it would if struck at the same speed and direction without English.

Round-robin. (General) A tournament format in which each contestant plays each of the other players once.

Run. (General) The total of consecutive scores, points or counts made by a player in one inning. The term is also used to indicate the total number of full short-rack games won without a missed shot in a match or tournament.

Running English. (General) Sidespin applied to the cue ball which causes it to rebound from an object ball or a cushion at a more acute angle and at a faster speed than it would if struck at the same speed and direction without English.

Safety. (General) Defensive positioning of the balls so as to minimize the opponent's chances to score. (The nature and rules concerning safety play are decidedly different in specific games; see individual game rules regarding safety play.) Player's inning ends after a safety play.

Scratch. (Carom games) To score a point largely by accident, due to an unanticipated kiss, unplanned time shot, etc.

Scratch. (Pocket games) The cue ball going into a pocket on a stroke.

Seeding. (General) Predetermined initial pairings or advanced positioning of players in a field of tournament competition.

Set. (General) Predetermined number of games necessary to win a match.

Shaft. (General) The thinner part of a cue, on which the cue tip is attached. On a two-piece cue, the shaft extends from the cue tip to the joint.

Shake bottle. (Pocket games) See *bottle*.

Shot. (General) An action that begins at the instant the cue tip contacts the cue ball, and ends when all balls in play stop rolling and spinning.

Short. (General) Usually refers to a ball which, due to stroke, travels a path with more narrow angles than those that are standard for a ball struck without English.

Short-rack. (Pocket games) Games which utilize less than fifteen object balls.

Single elimination. (General) A tournament format in which a single loss eliminates a player from the competition.

Snake. (Carom games) A shot in which the use of English causes the cue ball to make three or more cushion contacts, though utilizing only two different cushions.

Snookerbed. (Snooker) The condition of incoming player's cue-ball position when he cannot shoot in a straight line and contact all portions of an on ball directly facing the cue ball (because of balls not "on" that block the path). (Included for information only, since the rules of American snooker in this book are of such nature that being snookered has no special impact on the game rules or play).

Snookered. (Snooker) When the cue ball is obstructed by a ball or balls not on, and it cannot be stroked in a direct line to any part of every ball on.

Split doubled elimination. (General) A modification of the double elimination tournament format, in which the field is divided into sections, with one player emerging from each of the sections to compete for the championship, in a single showdown match for the championship.

Split hit. (General) A shot in which it cannot be determined which object ball(s) the cue ball contacted first, due to the close proximity of the object balls.

Spot. (General) The thin, circular piece of cloth or paper glued onto the cloth to indicate the spot locals (i.e., head spot, center spot, foot spot). Also an expression to describe a handicap.

Spot ball. (Carom games) The white ball differentiated from the clear by one or more markings; usually spots, dots or circles.

Spot shot. (Pocket games) Player shoots a ball on the foot spot with the cue ball in hand behind the head string.

Spotting balls. (General) Replacing balls to the table in positions as dictated by specific game rules.

Stance. (General) The position of the body during shooting. (See chapter 4).

Stop shot. (Pocket games) A shot in which the cue ball stops immediately upon striking the object ball.

Striker. (Snooker) The player who is about to shoot and has yet to complete his inning.

Stroke. (General) The movement of the cue as a shot is executed. (See chapter 4).

Successive fouls. (Pocket games) Fouls made on consecutive strokes by the same player, also called consecutive fouls.

Table in position. (General) Term used to indicate that the object balls remain unmoved following a shot.

Throw shot. (Pocket games) 1. A cut shot that alters the path of the ball by applying English. 2. A combination shot of frozen or near frozen object balls that is struck by the cue ball left or right of center on the first object ball, thus causing the second (or played) object ball to travel in the opposite direction of the cue-ball hit.

Time shot. (General) A shot in which the cue ball (most often) moves another ball into a different position and then continues on to meet one of the transposed balls for a score.

Top cushion. (Snooker) The cushion located at the foot of a snooker table, closest to the black spot.

Triangle. (Pocket games) The triangular device used to place the balls in position for the start of most games.

Yellow ball. (Carom games) In international competition the spot ball has been replaced by a yellow ball without any markings.

INSTRUCTIONAL PLAYING TIPS

4

There are many variations of the game of billiards, but the fundamentals of good billiard playing are inherent in every form of the sport. This section deals with these fundamentals.

CUES

Cue Selection. Try several cues and start with one that feels most comfortable to you. It is difficult for a beginning pool player to know which weight of a cue to get. Keep in mind that most professional pool players use a cue that is between 18 to 20 ounces. The shaft size of a cue has to do mainly with personal preference and the size of your fingers. Shaft sizes for pool cues basically run between 12 and 14 millimeters. Most professional pool players play with a shaft size of 12½ to 13½ millimeters.

Proper Grip of a Cue. Hold the cue lightly with the thumb and first three fingers (figure 4–1). When the cue is gripped properly, it should not touch the palm of your hand (figure 4–2). It is very important to maintain a light grip on the cue at all times. Gripping the cue too tightly while stroking through the cue ball is a common mistake that must be corrected.

Where to Grip the Cue. When you are bent over in your shooting position and the cue tip is almost touching the cue ball, the shooting hand should be directly under the elbow. It is okay to have the shoot-

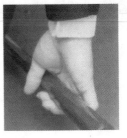

FIGURE 4–1   FIGURE 4–2

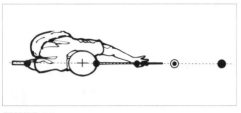

FIGURE 4–3

ing hand an inch or two ahead of the elbow at impact. It is never recommended to have the shooting hand behind the elbow at impact (figure 4–3).

Cue Stance.   Face the shot. Before you bend over to shoot, line up three points: your chin, the cue ball, and the exact place you want the cue ball to go. Turn your body slightly to the right without your chin leaving the line. Bend over at the waist, put your bridge hand down seven to ten inches from the cue ball so that your chin is two to eight inches directly above the cue stick. Adjust your feet to distribute your body weight approximately fifty-fifty (as shown in figure 4–4). When in your shooting position, a generally accepted stance is when the tip of the right toe is directly under the line of the cue and the left toe is slightly to the left side of the line of the cue. This should allow a four-to-six-inch gap between the hip and the cue for freedom of movement.

A common mistake made by beginners in their shooting position is having the shoulders and chest facing the cue ball. A preferred technique is to turn the left shoulder out in front and the right shoulder back thus turning the chest more to the right. This gives a better body alignment (figure 4–5).

FIGURE 4–5

FIGURE 4–4

BRIDGES.   One of the most overlooked fundamentals of the game is a solid bridge. The difference between a good billiard player and just another billiard player can most often be traced to their bridges. Nothing is of greater importance in billiard play. If the shot you are executing is to be accurate, your bridge must be natural, yet give firm guidance to the cue.

There are two basic bridges—an open bridge and a closed bridge.

Open Bridge. An open bridge is formed by placing the hand firmly on the table, cupping the hand, pressing the thumb against the forefinger forming a "V" (figure 4–6). The cue is now placed on the "V" (figure 4–7). To adjust the height of the bridge, simply pull the fingers toward you raising the bridge (figure 4–8), or pushing the fingers away to lower the bridge (figure 4–9). This allows you to strike the cue ball high, medium or low while maintaining a solid bridge. This bridge is highly recommended for beginners. Professionals use this bridge on many shots that don't require a lot of power or cue-ball spin.

FIGURE 4–6

FIGURE 4–7

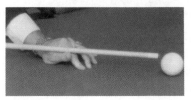

FIGURE 4–8

FIGURE 4–9

Stretch Shots. When stretching out for a shot where a long bridge is required (twelve inches or more), it is very important to use an open bridge. Keep the backswing and follow-through very short and use minimum speed (figure 4–10).

FIGURE 4–10

Standard (Closed) Bridge. Place your bridge hand flat on the table. The heel of your hand should be firmly down (figure 4–11). Bend

FIGURE 4-11

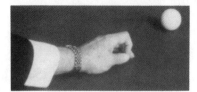

FIGURE 4-12

your forefinger so that its tip touches your thumb, forming a loop (figure 4-12). Place the cue tip in the loop formed by forefinger and thumb, resting the cue against the inner groove of these two fingers. Extend the cue through the loop formed by the above. Now pull your forefinger firmly against the cue, but with the loop just loose enough so that you can stroke the cue back and forth easily. As you do the above, keep your middle, ring and small fingers spread out and firmly pressed against the table. They form the bridge tripod which must be firm, yet natural. You have the correct bridge when the cues passes through easily and accurately, with firm guidance and support.

The bridge length is the distance between the loop of the forefinger and the cue ball on a closed bridge, or the thumb and the cue ball on an open bridge. Most professional pool players use a bridge length of seven to ten inches. Whether you use an open or a closed bridge, the heel of your hand should be firmly on the table at all times. The bridge hand must not move while you are striking the ball.

Bridge for Follow Shot. Using a standard bridge, elevate the tripod fingers slightly. Keep the cue level (figure 4-13).

Bridge for Draw Shot. Using the standard bridge, lower the tripod fingers until your thumb rests on the bed of the table. Keep the cue level (figure 4-14).

FIGURE 4-13

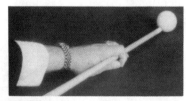

FIGURE 4-14

Rail Bridges. If the cue ball is four inches or more away from the rail, set your bridge hand on the rail. Place your thumb under the index finger (figure 4-15). Put the cue on the rail against the thumb, and bring your forefinger over the shaft (figure 4-16). Keep your cue as level as possible when stroking your shot.

If the cue ball is closer than four inches from the rail, place the cue between the thumb and forefinger. Place the other three fingers on the rail (as shown in figure 4-17).

FIGURE 4-15

FIGURE 4-16

FIGURE 4-17

Bridge for Over-Ball Shot. When it is necessary to shoot over an object ball in order to stroke the cue ball, the following bridge should be employed. Bracing all four of your fingers on the bed of the table behind the obstructing object ball(s), raise the hand as high as necessary and place the cue on the support made by your index finger joint and the thumb (figures 4–18 and 4–19). This is an uncomfortable bridge, but a very necessary one, which should be practiced.

FIGURE 4-18

FIGURE 4-19

FIGURE 4-20

Mechanical Bridges. If a shot is beyond reach with any of the above-mentioned bridges, a mechanical bridge should be employed. Don't sacrifice a shot because you cannot use the mechanical bridge: it is very easy. Set the bridge on the table six to eight inches from the cue ball. Place your hand on the bridge. Place the shaft of your cue in the notch at the front of the bridge. (Use the higher notch to "follow," lower notch to "draw" or "stop.") Place your thumb under the base of the cue and your four fingers over the top of the cue. Your elbow will be sticking out to the side as you stroke; the bridge will be to the left if you are right-handed. Be sure to lay the bridge flat on the table if possible (figure 4–20) and secure it with your left hand. Now use the same system as for any other shot.

LEARNING A STROKE

Remember, "Practice doesn't make perfect; *perfect practice* makes perfect." A stroke is a throwing motion. A good throwing motion starts with a slow backswing with a smooth acceleration through the cue ball. A common mistake by amateur and beginning players is to drop the elbow while stroking through the cue ball. It's important to note that the throwing motion must only take place in that part of the arm below the elbow. The less the elbow moves up and down, the more precise the stroke. It should be a pendulum swing from the elbow down.

CUEING THE BALL

For the beginning player, it is important to adjust the bridge so that the cue tip strikes the cue ball a little above center, never to the left or right, while he is learning accuracy and speed control. As his skill level progresses, it will be necessary for him to learn to strike the cue ball at other places—higher, lower, left, right, etc.

The most important things to learn after a player has progressed past the beginner stage are how to make the cue ball follow, how to stop your cue ball on a straight-in shot, and how to make the cue ball draw or reverse direction off the object ball. The smoother the stroke, the lower or higher the cue ball may be struck without miscueing. Most good players can strike the cue ball almost two full tips off center without miscueing.

Keep in mind that extreme spin requires a very good stroke and smooth delivery. When following the cue ball, the higher the tip strikes the cue ball, the more overspin will be pushed on the cue ball. Likewise for backspin: The lower you shoot the cue ball, the more backspin is imparted to the cue ball by the cue tip. In pool there is one stroke. You use the same stroke to follow, stop or draw the cue ball.

A common mistake is that when players want to stop or draw the cue ball, they think they have to jab or hit the cue ball and stop the cue tip immediately on impact, or even hit the cue ball and pull the stick back. That is not the way to stop or draw the cue ball. To make the cue ball stop, you must put enough backspin on it by shooting below center to cause it to arrive at the object ball with no spin. The cloth is always trying to rub the backspin off the cue ball. The farther the cue ball is from the object ball, the lower and/or harder you must shoot to cause the cue ball to stop or come back (figure 4–21 shows positions 1–4 for moderate spin, and 5–8 for

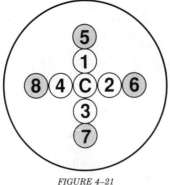

FIGURE 4–21

FIGURE 4–22

extreme spin). It is important to understand that the backspin you put on the cue ball is caused by the tremendous friction the chalk creates between the tip and the cue ball. The cue stick pushes backspin on the cue ball as you throw it four to six inches through the lower part of the cue ball. Figure 4–22 shows how the cue stick follows through four to six inches after contact with the object ball.

HITTING THE OBJECT BALL

The first thing the pocket-billiard player must learn is that his eyes should be on the object ball as he executes the shot. During the aiming process his eyes go back and forth between the cue ball and the object ball. When you are ready to pocket the object ball, your eyes are on the object ball.

To shoot a ball into a pocket, the simplest way to determine your point of impact on the object ball is to draw an imaginary line from the center of the pocket which bisects the object ball. Where this line extends through the object ball is your contact point, the point at which the edge of the cue ball must contact the edge of the object ball. You must aim so that these two contact points will meet (figure 4–23).

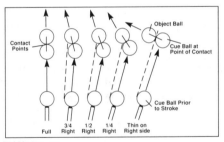

FIGURE 4–23

POINT OF AIM, POINT OF IMPACT

In figures 4–24 and 4–25, you can see there is a white dot on the object ball. This mark is where the cue ball must contact the object ball in order to pocket the ball. The white dot is called the point of

FIGURE 4–24

FIGURE 4–25

impact. The white dot on the table is the point of aim. No matter where the cue ball is, the cue stick and the center of the cue ball are aimed at the point of aim in order to contact the point of impact on the object ball.

A keen eye and judgment are important here. Your skill in hitting the point of aim will determine your status in pocket-billiard circles.

Once again there is no better experience than practice. Accomplish this phase by placing your cue ball close to the object ball, then gradually increase the distance between the two balls. Time and practice will increase your accuracy in striking the cue ball correctly and hitting the object ball where you aim, thus driving it to the exact target area.

LEARNING A GOOD SHOOTING SYSTEM

The first thing to remember when you play pool is that you don't control the balls. All you control is your body and cue stick. What the balls do is a result of how well your body moves the cue stick. There are two things you have to make sure of before you can shoot any shot: that the cue is aiming straight and that your arm can move the cue straight back and forth the full length of your bridge (seven to ten inches).

A good practice technique is to place the cue ball on the spot and shoot it down the table into a corner pocket. Be sure to get your stance and aim correct. Then take a couple of smooth, slow warm-up swings the full length of the bridge. Stop at the cue ball and check your aim by letting your eyes go down the line of the cue stick to the target and back a couple of times. If the aim looks perfect, lock your eyes on the target, then after a slow backswing, throw the cue stick smoothly four to six inches through the cue ball directly over the dot. If after executing the shot, the cue stick is to the left or right of the dot, repeat this system until you can shoot the ball into the pocket and the cue stick finishes its motion four to six inches straight ahead and directly over the dot. It is imperative that the head remain perfectly still during the shot. This is an important practice technique to help in developing your accuracy and stroke.

The warm-up swings should be slow and smooth in both directions, training the arm to make the cue go straight. After every two or three warm-up strokes, be sure to stop the cue ball and check the aim. If it looks perfect, take a smooth backswing, and then accelerate four to six inches through the cue ball at any speed you want to shoot. It is very important that you always maintain the same slow backswing no matter how hard you accelerate through the ball. Never go back faster just because you want to shoot harder. It's just like throwing a ball; to be accurate, you go back slowly, then you throw hard.

Learn to stroke through the ball at all speeds. Although you have more control at slower speeds, sometimes position play will require you to shoot a ball harder. Keep in mind—slow backswing, accelerate forward.

ENGLISH

When we talk about *english,* we are generally referring to left or right spin on the cue ball. By putting left or right spin on the cue ball, you immediately do three things that can cause you to miss a shot. Beginning with right-hand English, when you strike the cue ball on the right-hand side, the cue ball immediately deflects off the tip to the left of the line of the cue stick. As the cue ball proceeds down the table, it may curve back to the right just a little bit. It will never curve back as much as it deflects unless you elevate the cue, which we're not going to talk about here. Lastly, the English might throw the object ball. Right-hand English can throw the object ball a little to the left of the contact line.

Thus the three things that happen when you use right-hand English: the deflection immediately off the tip, the curve back to the right, and the throwing of the object ball to the left. Of these three, the curve is usually very slight. The throwing of the object ball is very slight. The biggest factor in causing people to miss with English is the deflection off the cue tip. It is important to remember when using right-hand English, aim slightly to the right of where you would normally aim on the object ball. When using left-hand English, you must aim slightly to the left of where you would normally aim on the object ball.

Left- or right-hand English is almost never used to pocket an object ball but rather for playing position on another object ball. The purpose of applying sidespin to the cue ball is to change the angle at which the cue ball comes off a rail after pocketing the object ball. Always remember never to use English to make balls, only to play position on the next ball. Although English is extremely important in playing position the pros will tell you the less English you use the less often you get in trouble (figure 4–26).

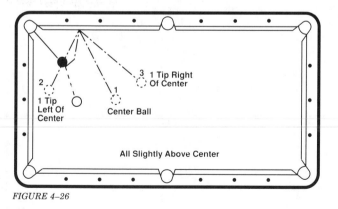

FIGURE 4–26

Follow Shots. Set up the balls as in figure 4–27. By stroking the cue ball between a tip and a tip and a half above center, the cue ball will follow to position 1. Then set up the same shot and stroke the cue ball

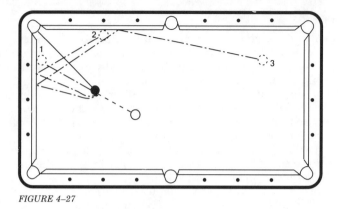

FIGURE 4-27

at the same height, add some power and see that the cue ball will end up in position 2. Now stroke the cue ball again in the same position, but with an even firmer stroke to see the cue ball respond as in position 3 in the figure.

Stop Shots. Place the balls on the table as in figure 4-28. Strike the cue ball about a tip below center. Use a smooth stroke and practice stopping the cue ball as it contacts the object ball. Do this a few times to get the feel of how hard you shoot, then practice shooting this same shot a little lower on the cue ball with a little less speed and see if you can still get the same results. Then place the cue ball at position 2. This time stroke the cue ball about a tip and a half below center and a little firmer than position 1. By repeating this practice in a new position, you will learn how much force you need in order to stop the cue ball. Continue this practice with the cue ball in positions 3 and 4, each time increasing the power of the stroke. If you have any difficulty at a particular position, repeat that practice until it feels comfortable. Remember, the lower you strike the cue ball, the less power is required to stop the cue ball on contact with the object ball.

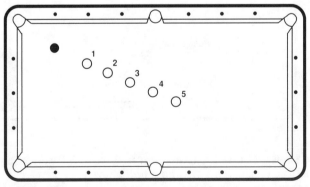

FIGURE 4-28

Draw Shots. Place the balls as shown in figure 4–29. Notice there is a slight angle in the ball placement so that when you draw the cue ball it will move over to the right slightly and then come back past your cue stick. The reason for this is so that you can follow through the cue ball four to six inches to practice a good follow-through on each shot without worrying about the cue ball hitting your stick. With the balls in position, strike the cue ball about a tip and a half below center with a moderate stroke and notice that the cue ball travels a couple of inches to the right of your stick before it travels a short distance down the table to position 1. By increasing the force of your stroke, you will be able to move the ball farther down the table toward positions 2 and 3. It is important on all these exercises to be sure the cue tip follows through four to six inches. For any stop or draw shot, the cue ball is struck one to one and a half tips below center. When the pendelum motion of the arm is correct, the cue tip will follow through four to six inches past the object ball, and continue in a slightly downward motion, ending up touching the cloth.

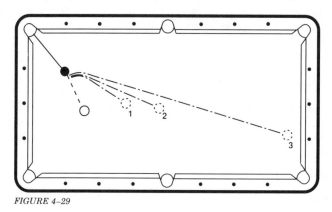

FIGURE 4–29

Position Play. Players are forever trying to play position. That is, making an easy shot and making the cue ball arrive at a place on the table to have another easy shot. The two secrets of playing proper position are memory and speed control. When a beginner is learning to play, he should repeat the same shots over and over. Not only do you watch the object ball being pocketed, but the path of the cue ball after contacting the object ball. If you are continually hitting the cue ball a little above center, the cue ball will always take virtually the same path. Fifty percent of position play is remembering where the cue ball went after that particular shot. The other fifty percent of position play is the speed control of the cue ball.

The most important and easiest way a beginner can learn position is to set up a shot (figure 4–29). When you set up a practice shot, mark the cloth with a dot of chalk under the object ball and the cue ball, so you start at the same position each time. Pocket the object ball by hitting a little above center and watch where the cue ball hits the first rail and the direction it takes coming off that rail. By

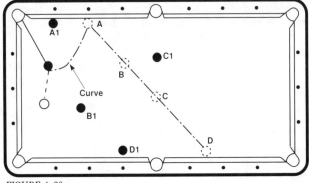

FIGURE 4–30

shooting this shot several times at different speeds, but striking the cue ball in the same spot each time, you will notice that the path of the cue ball follows the same line each time you shoot. To improve your game, work on playing position on each of the shots in the diagram by varying the speed in which you strike the cue ball.

Now if you set the balls up in the same position and strike the cue ball a little below center, you will notice that the path of the cue ball will be completely different off the object ball. Repeat this several times, until you can make the cue ball go in the same direction, but travel farther down the table depending on the speed of your stroke. After setting up these shots and hitting the ball a little below center, set them up and strike the cue ball even farther below center. This is a good exercise to learn the basics of what happens when you shoot the cue ball at different heights and speeds.

EXERCISES

Follow, Stop and Draw. This exercise shows you the different ways the cue ball will react when it is cued at different levels. Set up the shot in figure 4–31. The object ball is about a diamond out and

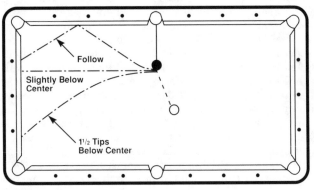

FIGURE 4–31

directly in line between the two side pockets. The cue ball is at a slight angle toward the diamond past the side pocket. When you hit the cue ball with follow, the cue ball will take a slight curve as shown in the path in the diagram. If you hit the cue ball slightly below center, if will go almost straight down the table. If the cue ball is hit about one and a half tips below center, it will curve back more toward the corner pocket.

Position Exercise. Learning position play is the easiest way to get the balls off the table. The best way to learn that is an exercise we call 3-Ball, Ball in Hand. This is one of the best exercises to improve your skill level in control and position. Throw three balls on the table. In figure 4–32, we see balls 1, 2, and 3. This numeric order is the easiest way to play off these balls by placing the cue ball as

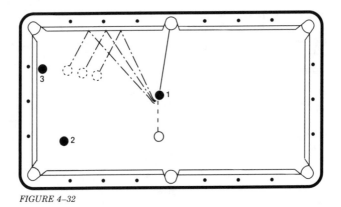

FIGURE 4–32

shown. Striking the cue ball above center on the 1 ball, you can see by the path of the cue ball that it will follow into the rail and then head right toward the 2 ball. By going to the rail after pocketing the 1 ball and depending on your speed of stroke, you can end up in any of the three cue-ball positions. It is very difficult to make a mistake. This is what pros look for: the easiest way to get position on their next ball. If you shoot the cue ball again above center and pocket the 2 ball, the cue balls ends up anywhere within the darkened quarter-circle around 2 ball. Then the 3 ball is an easily pocketed shot.

One of the best ways of improving your game of pool is by repeating shots. Don't repeat long, difficult shots. The ones to repeat are the easy and semieasy ones that are frequently missed. For the more proficient players, even if you make the object ball and fail to get position, repeat that same shot until you feel comfortable that you can make that ball and get position.

Most people think that if they could make tough shots, they would be better players. The reality is that games are not won by people who make the tough shots; games are lost by players who miss shots that are very easy.

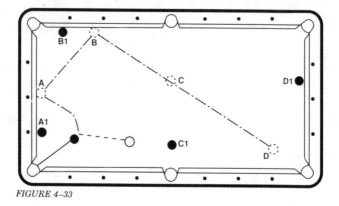

FIGURE 4–33

Figure 4–33 shows the many ways the speed of stroke can be used to play position. By suing a soft stroke, you can play to position A to play A1 for your next shot. A slightly harder stroke will go to position B for B1 as the next shot. Continue working on your speed of stroke until you can play position on shots C1 and D1.

Eight Ball and Nine Ball, Ball in Hand.   Another great practice technique for beginners or stronger players is to play eight-ball or nine-ball with a rule change. When a person breaks and a ball is made on the break, he can take "ball in hand" anywhere on the table and shoot until he misses. The incoming player also takes ball in hand and shoots until he misses. The advantage of playing this way is that when you have ball in hand every time you come to the table, you start looking over the table. Even a beginner will start to see patterns of two or maybe three balls. The better player learns very quickly the easiest way to run the balls off. It trains you to see patterns and the easy way to go for a run out. By playing ball-in-hand pool whether it is eight-ball or nine-ball, you learn in one hour the equivalent of what you would learn in about fifteen hours of regular practice.

Ball-in-Hand Equal Offense.   Another great practice game is a variation of equal offense, covered elsewhere in this book. In equal offense, each ball is one point and you can shoot at any ball. No balls count on the break. After the break, the same player that breaks gets ball in hand three times per rack. After each miss, he gets ball in hand again. Then he records how many balls he made that rack. A perfect score is 150 points in ten racks. By playing this three-miss way, a person learns to see and play simple patterns. When a person's score approaches 130 or more in ten racks, then he progresses to the two-miss level. Now he breaks the balls and after the break, he gets ball in hand twice per rack. When his score improves again to 130 or more in ten racks, then he is playing well enough to progress to the one-miss level. Any player who shoots 130 points or more on the one-miss level is a very good amateur player.

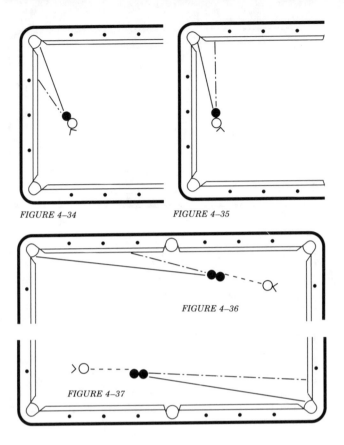

FIGURE 4-34

FIGURE 4-35

FIGURE 4-36

FIGURE 4-37

Throw Shots. Figures 4–34 to 4–37. The object of a throw shot is to provide force or English that will move an object ball along an off-center path, when two balls are frozen.

This situation often arises when the cue ball is touching (frozen to) an object ball. If the two are in alignment with a pocket, there is no problem. If not in alignment, it is still possible to pocket the object ball by using a throw shot which spins the object ball to the left or right. Figure 4–34 shows how, by hitting the cue ball on the left side, the object ball is thrown to the right side. Figure 4–35 illustrates that striking the cue ball on the right side will move the object ball to the left.

Another version of the throw shot is when two object balls are frozen together. The cue ball is free, but not in position to pocket either ball easily. In this case, the cue ball (hit without English) strikes the closest object ball on either the right side (figure 4–36) or the left side (figure 4–37) to throw the second object ball in the opposite direction.

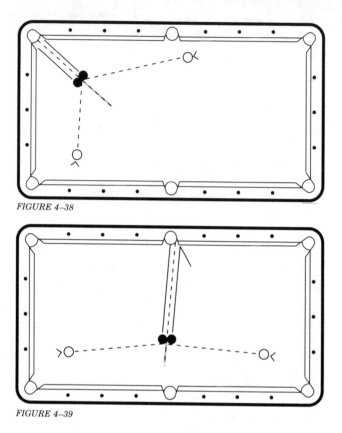

FIGURE 4–38

FIGURE 4–39

Kiss Shots. Figures 4–38 and 4–39 The object of this exercise is to pocket one of two balls that are frozen together without the use of English. When two balls are frozen together, an axis or center line is established by their relationship. A cue extended along this imaginary line will readily determine if the closest object ball, when struck on the back half, will follow the line into a pocket. If the cue does not point to a pocket, the object ball will not go into a pocket.

Figure 4–38 shows how this kiss shot can be made from either side. Figure 4–39 demonstrates that one object ball can be pocketed. The other cannot. Arrange two balls into various frozen positions and practice finding the center line. Then, mix throw shots with kiss shots to increase your options under these conditions.

RULES FOR TOURNAMENT PLAY

The following rules concern the play, scoring, officiating and responsibilities for tournament competition in both pocket and carom games. However, the precepts and principles of these rules are to be considered part of the games' general rules, and should be applied to all play, whether or not a formal tournament.

1. PLAYER RESPONSIBILITY. It is the player's responsibility to be aware of all rules, regulations and schedules applying to his competition. While tournament officials will make every reasonable effort to have such information readily available to all players, the ultimate responsibility rests with the player. Though referees may do their best to advise all players of certain traditional and factual situations during play (such as being "on two fouls" in 14.1, or being "on one" or "on two fouls" in nine ball), once again the player has no recourse if such information is not volunteered.

2. ACCEPTANCE OF EQUIPMENT. Tournament players should assure themselves, prior to beginning play, that the balls and other equipment are standard and legal. Once they begin play of a match, they may no longer question the legality of the equipment in use, unless the opponent and tournament officials both agree with the objection and any available remedy proposed by the tournament officials.

3. USE OF EQUIPMENT. Players may not use equipment or accessory items for purposes, or in a manner, other than those for which the items were intended. For example, powder containers, chalk cubes, etc., may not be used to prop up a mechanical bridge (or natural hand bridge); no more than two mechanical bridges may be used at one time, nor may they be used to support anything other than the cue shaft. Extra or out-of-play balls may not be used by players to check clearances or for any other reason (except to lag for break). The triangle may not be employed by players to ascertain whether a ball is in the rack unless a match is unofficiated and the table has not been pencil-marked around the triangle area.

Tournament officials should prevent these actions from occurring. Generally, no penalty is applied, because the referee or other tournament official intercedes prior to that point. However, should a player persist in activity counter to any general rule after having been advised that the activity is not permissible, tournament officials may take action against him as appropriate under the provisions of unsportsmanlike conduct.

4. EQUIPMENT RESTRICTIONS. Players may use chalk, powder, mechanical bridge(s) and cue of their choice and/or design. However, tournament officials may restrict a player if he attempts action that is disruptive of either the house equipment or normal competitive conditions. As examples, a player may be restrained from using blue chalk on gold cloth; he may be advised not to use powder in such an excessive fashion as to unduly affect the balls or table cloth; he may be barred from using a cue with a noise-making device that is clearly disruptive to other competitors.

5. MARKING OF TABLES. Prior to competition, each table and the triangle to be used on it shall be marked so as to ensure that the same triangle will be used throughout the tournament on the same table.

An accurate and clearly visible pencil line must also be marked on the cloth: around the outer edge of the triangle to ensure accurate and consistent placement and to enable accurate judgment as to ball positions; on the long string to enable accurate spotting of balls; and on the head string to determine whether balls are behind the head string.

The head spot, center spot and foot spot must also be accurately marked, whether with discreet penciled "plus" marks, or with standard spots if being employed.

6. ADMINISTRATIVE DISCRETION. The management of each tournament shall reserve the right to set forth rules and procedures appropriate and reasonable for the particular tournament involved, such as may regard players' dress requirements, methods of receiving entry fees, refund policy of entry fees, scheduling flexibility, pairing procedures, etc.

However, for tournaments to receive a BCA sanction, certain requirements must be met, primarily with regard to safeguarding and ensuring proper distribution of the prize fund.

7. SCORING OF FORFEITS. Matches forfeited for any reason under these rules shall not result in any scores being included in the statistics of a tournament, regardless of whether any score had been reached prior to the declaration of forfeiture. For official records, no point scores should be recorded, but rather the notations "W(F)" and "L(F)" as appropriate should be employed. Matches lost through disqualification are considered forfeits for purposes of this rule.

If, however, the player awarded a match through his opponent's forfeiture has posted a high run (or similar accomplishment for which an award is granted) during play of the match prior to declaration of forfeiture, that high run or other mark shall be eligible for the tournament award or prize.

(Note: U.S.B.A. three-cushion rules differ; see specific game rules.)

INSTRUCTIONS FOR REFEREES

1. TOURNAMENT OFFICIALS/REFEREES. Where these rules refer to a "referee," it should be noted that the referee's prerogatives and discretion also accrue to other tournament officials as appropriate.

2. REFEREE'S AUTHORITY. The referee will maintain order and enforce the rules of the game. He is the final judge in all matters of fact. The referee is in complete charge of the match he is officiating. He may, at his discretion, consult other tournament officials for rule interpretation, ball positions, etc. However, all matters of judgment are his and his alone; they cannot be appealed to higher tournament authority by players. Only if the referee is in error on a rule or its application, may higher tournament authority overrule him.

3. REFEREE'S RESPONSIVENESS. The referee shall be totally responsive to players' inquiries regarding objective data, such as whether a ball will be in the rack, if a ball is in the kitchen, what the count is, how many points are needed for a victory, if a player is playing from safety, if a player or his opponent is on a foul, what rule would apply if a certain shot is made, etc. However, he must not offer or provide any subjective opinion that would affect play, such as whether a good hit can be made on a prospective shot, whether a combination is makeable, how the table seems to be playing, etc.

4. FINAL TOURNAMENT AUTHORITY. Though these rules attempt to cover the vast majority of situations that arise in competition, there still may be an occasional need for interpretation of the rules and their proper application under unusual circumstances. The tournament director or other official who assumes final responsibility for a tournament will make any such required decision (other than referee's judgment calls) at his discretion, and they shall be final.

5. WAGERING BY REFEREES. Referees are strictly prohibited from wagering of any kind involving the games, players or tournament. Any such wagering by a referee (or other tournament official) shall result in his immediate dismissal and the forfeiture of his entire financial compensation for the tournament.

6. BEFORE THE MATCH. Before the match, the referee will clean the table and balls if necessary. He will ensure that chalk and mechanical bridges are available. He will mark the head string and long string with a pencil, if they are not already marked.

7. RACKING. The referee will rack the ball as tightly as possible, which means each ball should be touching its neighbors. Tapping a ball into place is not recommended. It is preferable to thoroughly brush the area of the rack to even out the cloth.

8. CALLING FOULS. The referee will call fouls as soon as they occur and will inform the incoming player that he has ball in hand in games where the rule applies.

9. CLEARING POCKETS. On tables that do not have ball return systems, the referee will remove pocketed object balls from full or nearly full pockets. It is the player's responsibility to see that this duty is performed; he has no recourse if a ball rebounds from a full pocket.

10. CLEANING BALLS. During a game a player may ask the referee to clean one or more balls. The referee will clean any visibly soiled ball.

11. SOLICITING INFORMATION. If the referee does not have a clear view of a possible foul, he may ask spectators for assistance in determining what occurred. The referee will then weigh all evidence as he sees fit.

12. WARNINGS WHICH ARE MANDATORY. The referee must warn a player who is about to commit a serious foul (such as three consecutive fouls, requesting coaching assistance, or failure to stop shooting after a foul has been called); otherwise any foul is considered to be a standard foul (except as specially noted). In games where the rule applies, the referee must warn a player who has had two consecutive fouls; otherwise the player is considered to have had only one foul prior to the shot. The referee must warn a player when an object ball is touching a rail; otherwise any contact on that ball is considered to have driven it to that rail. The referee should issue warnings as soon as the corresponding situation arises. A warning given just as a shot starts is not considered sufficient; the player must be given enough time to react.

13. RESTORING A POSITION. When it becomes necessary, the referee will restore disturbed balls to their original positions to the best of his ability. The referee may ask for information for this purpose if he is not sure of the original position.

If the balls were disturbed by a player, the other player has the option of preventing the restoration. In this case, the referee should clearly indicate where the balls will be moved to if they are restored, and only restore the balls if requested to do so.

14. OUTSIDE INTERFERENCE. When outside interference occurs during a shot that has an effect on the outcome of that shot, the referee will restore the balls to the positions they had before the shot, and the shot will be replayed. If the interference had no effect on the shot, the referee will restore the disturbed balls and play will continue. If the balls cannot be restored to their original position, replay the game with the original player breaking.

15. ILLEGALLY CAUSING BALL TO MOVE. Any player who, in the referee's judgment, intentionally moves a ball by illegal means (pushing on bed cloth, bumping or slapping table, etc.) will lose the game and/or match by forfeit (referee's judgment and discretion under the rules of unsportsmanlike conduct).

16. OUT OF HEAD STRING WARNING. When player has the *cue ball in hand behind the head string,* the referee shall warn him before he shoots if he has not placed it within the head string. If the player shoots on or outside the string after having been warned of the legal placement, the stroke is a foul. See specific game rules for penalty.

17. REMAINING IN PLAYER'S CHAIR. Players are to remain in the chair designated for their use while opponent is at the table. Should a player need to leave the playing area during matches, he must request and receive permission from the referee. The referee shall apply his good judgment to ensure that undue time is not being used or that a player is not abusing the privilege as a means of unsettling an opponent.

18. OUTSIDE ASSISTANCE PROHIBITED. Unless specifically permitted by the rules of a given tournament, players may not knowingly accept any form of playing advice during a match. A player may not engage in communication, either verbal or nonverbal, with persons other than the tournament officials or his opponent during play.

Should a player desire to so communicate, for example to obtain a beverage, get a piece of equipment, or other permissible reason, he should either communicate through a tournament official or with the approval and observance of the referee.

If the referee has reason to believe that a player knowingly solicited or accepted outside assistance in any manner regarding the play of a match, he shall take steps appropriate under the provisions of unsportsmanlike conduct.

19. NONPLAYER INTERFERENCE OR HARASSMENT. If a nonplayer either verbally or visually interferes with the players, the referee may request that he leave the playing area.

20. SLOW PLAY. If in the opinion of the referee a player is impeding the progress of the tournament or game with consistently slow play, the referee can warn the player and then at his discretion impose a one-minute time limit for that person between shots. If the referee does impose a one-minute time limit and that limit is exceeded, a foul will be called and the incoming player will be rewarded according to the rules applicable to the game being played.

21. PROTESTS. A player may request a rule interpretation or application from the referee or appropriate tournament authority. He must, however, make such a request or protest immediately, prior to any subsequent shot being taken, or it cannot be considered or honored.

All players must honor an opponent's request that play be halted if an official is to be summoned or if a referee is to check or verify a rule question with other officials. Failure to honor such requests may result in disqualification or forfeiture under the provisions of unsportsmanlike conduct.

22. SUSPENDING PLAY. The referee has the authority to suspend play during protests by players and whenever he feels that conditions are unsuitable for play to continue. If a spectator is interfering with the game, play may be suspended until that spectator is removed from the area.

23. UNSPORTSMANLIKE CONDUCT. The referee has the right and obligation to ensure that no player engages in any activity which, in his judgment, is unsportsmanlike in nature, embarrassing, disruptive or detrimental to other players, tournament officials or hosts, or the sport in general. The referee or other officials shall have the right to penalize or disqualify, with or without warning, any player who conducts himself in an unsportsmanlike manner.

GENERAL RULES OF POCKET BILLIARDS

The rules included in this section apply generally to all the specific varieties of pocket-billiard games included in this rulebook. These general rules apply to all pocket-billiard games, *unless* specifically noted to the contrary in the individual game rules.

To facilitate the use and understanding of these general rules, terms that may require definition are set in *italics* so that the reader may refer to the Glossary of Billiard Terms chapter for the exact meaning of the term.

For purposes of simplicity and clarity, masculine pronouns have been utilized throughout this rule book. Such references apply to any player or teams of players.

1. TABLES, BALLS, EQUIPMENT. All games described in this rule book are designed for tables, balls and equipment meeting the standards prescribed in chapter 2.

2. STRIKING CUE BALL. Legal shots require that the *cue ball* be struck only with the *cue tip*. Failure to meet this requirement is a *foul*.

3. LAG FOR BREAK. The following procedure is used for the *lag* for the *opening break*. Each player should use balls of equal size and weight (preferably cue balls but, when not available, non-striped object balls). With the balls in hand behind the *head string,* one player to the left and one to the right of the *head spot,* the balls are shot simultaneously to the *foot cushion* and back to the head end of the table. The player whose ball is the closest to the innermost edge of the head cushion wins the lag. The lagged ball must contact the foot cushion at least once. Other cushion contacts are immaterial, except as prohibited below.

It is an automatic loss of the lag if: the ball crosses into the opponent's half of the table, or the ball fails to contact the foot cushion, or the ball drops into a pocket, or the ball *jumps* the table. If both players violate automatic-loss lag rules, or if the referee is unable to determine which ball is closer, the lag is a tie and is replayed.

4. OPENING BREAK SHOT. The opening break shot is determined by either lag or *lot*. (The lag-for-break procedure is required for tournament and other formal competition). The player winning the lag or lot has the choice of performing the opening break shot or assigning it to the opponent.

The position of the cue ball on opening break is in hand behind the head string. The object balls are positioned according to specific game rules.

5. CUE BALL ON OPENING BREAK. The *opening break shot* is taken with *cue ball in hand behind the string*. The object balls are positioned according to specific game rules.

6. CUE BALL IN HAND BEHIND THE STRING. When the cue ball is *in hand behind the string,* it remains in hand (not in play) until the player drives the cue ball out of the kitchen by striking it with his cue tip, or in the referee's judgment touches it with any part of the cue in an obvious attempt to perform a shot.

The cue ball may be adjusted by the player's hand, cue, etc., so long as it remains in hand. Once the cue ball is in play as defined above, it may not be impeded in any way by the player; to do so is to commit a foul.

7. POCKETED BALLS. A ball is considered as a pocketed ball if, as a result of a legal shot, it drops off the bed of the table into the pocket and remains there. (A ball that drops out of a ball-return system onto the floor is not to be construed as a ball that has not remained pocketed.) A ball that rebounds from a pocket back onto the table bed is not a pocketed ball.

8. POSITION OF BALLS. The position of a ball is judged by where its base (or center) rests.

9. FOOT ON FLOOR. It is a foul if a player shoots when at least one foot is not in contact with the floor. Foot attire must be normal in regard to size, shape and manner in which it is worn.

10. SHOOTING WITH BALLS IN MOTION. It is a foul if a player shoots while the cue ball or any object ball is in motion. A spinning ball is in motion.

11. COMPLETION OF STROKE. A stroke is not complete, and therefore is not counted, until all balls on the table have become motionless after the stroke.

12. KITCHEN DEFINED. The *head string* is not part of the *kitchen*. Thus an object that is dead center on the head string is playable when specific game rules require that a player must shoot at a ball outside of the kitchen. Likewise, the cue ball when being put in play from the kitchen (cue ball in hand behind the string), may not be placed directly on the head string; it must be behind it.

13. GENERAL RULE, ALL FOULS. Though the penalties for fouls differ from game to game, the following apply to all fouls: the player's inning ends, and if on a stroke, the stroke is invalid and any pocketed balls are not counted to the shooter's credit.

14. FOULS BY TOUCHING BALLS. Unless otherwise stated, it is a foul to strike, touch or in any way make contact with the cue ball in play or any object balls in play with anything (the body, clothing, chalk, mechanical bridge, cue shaft, etc.) except the cue tip (while attached to the cue shaft), which may contact the cue ball in the execution of a legal shot.

15. FOULS BY DOUBLE HITS. It is a foul if the cue ball is struck more than once on a shot by the cue tip. Such shots are usually referred to as *double hits*. If, in the referee's judgment, the cue ball has left initial contact with the cue tip and then is struck a second time in the course of the same stroke, it shall be a foul. (Note: This can be a difficult call in officiating, because on shots where the distance between the cue ball and the object ball is very short, the referee must judge whether the cue ball had time to move out of contact with the cue tip prior to being impeded, and then propelled again by the follow-through of the stroke. Nonetheless, if it is judged, by virtue of sound, ball position and action, and stroke used, that there were two separate contacts of the cue ball by the cue tip on a stroke, the stroke is a foul.

16. PUSH–SHOT FOULS. It is a foul if the cue ball is pushed by the cue tip, with contact being maintained for more than the momentary time commensurate with a stroked shot. Such shots are usually referred to as *push shots*. If, in the referee's judgment, the player lays the cue tip against the cue ball and then pushes on into the shot, maintaining contact beyond the normal momentary split second, the stroke is a foul.

17. PLAYER RESPONSIBILITY FOULS. The player is responsible for chalk, bridges, files and any other items or equipment he brings to, uses at, or causes to approximate the table. If he drops a piece of chalk, or knocks off a mechanical bridge head, as examples, he is guilty of a foul should such an object make contact with a cue ball or object ball in play.

18. CUE BALL JUMPED OFF TABLE. When a stroke results in the cue ball being a *jumped ball* off the table, the stroke is a foul. (Note: Jumped object balls may or may not be fouls; see specific game rules.)

19. ILLEGAL JUMPING OF BALL. It is a foul if a player strikes the cue ball below center ("digs under" it) and intentionally causes it to rise off the bed of the table in an effort to clear an obstructing ball. Such jumping action may occasionally occur accidentally, and such jumps are not to be considered fouls; they may still be ruled foul strokes, if for example, the ferrule or cue shaft makes contact with the cue ball in the course of the shot.

20. JUMP SHOTS. Unless otherwise stated in rules for a specific game it is legal to cause the cue ball to rise off the bed of the table by elevating the cue stick on the shot, and forcing the cue ball to rebound from the bed of the table.

21. BALLS JUMPED OFF TABLE. Balls coming to rest other than on the bed of the table after a stroke (on the cushion top, rail surface, floor, etc.) are considered jumped balls. Balls may bounce on the cushion tops, rails or light fixtures of the table in play without being jumped balls if they return to the bed of the table under their own power and without touching anything not a part of the table equipment. The table equipment shall consist of its light fixture, chalk not on the bed of the table, and permanent parts of the table proper. Balls that strike or touch anything not a part of the table equipment shall be considered jumped balls even though they might return to the bed of the table after contacting the nonequipment item[s].

All jumped object balls are spotted when all balls have stopped moving. See specific game rules to determine whether a jumped object ball is a foul. A cue ball jumped off the table is a foul; see specific game rules for putting the cue ball in play after a jumped cue ball foul.

22. SPECIAL INTENTIONAL FOUL PENALTY. The cue ball in play shall not be intentionally struck with anything other than a cue's attached tip (such as the ferrule, shaft, etc.). While such contact is automatically a foul under the provisions of Rule 13, if the referee deems the contact to be intentional, he shall warn the player once during a match that a second violation during that match will result in the loss of the match by forfeiture.

23. ONE FOUL LIMIT. Unless specific game rules dictate otherwise, only one foul is assessed on a player in each inning; if different penalties can apply, the most severe penalty is the factor determining which foul is assessed.

24. BALLS MOVING SPONTANEOUSLY. If a ball shifts, settles, turns or otherwise moves "by itself," the ball shall remain in the position it assumed and play continues. A hanging ball that falls into a pocket by itself after being motionless for five seconds or longer shall be replaced as closely as possible to its position prior to falling, and play shall continue.

If an object ball drops into a pocket by itself as a player shoots at it, so that the cue ball passes over the spot the ball had been on, unable to hit it, the cue ball and object ball are to be replaced to their positions prior to the stroke and the player must execute the shot again. Any other object balls disturbed on the stroke are also to be replaced to their original positions for the shot to be replayed.

25. SPOTTING BALLS. When specific game rules call for spotting balls, they shall be replaced on the table on the *long string* after the stroke is complete. A single ball is placed on the foot spot; if more than one ball is to be spotted, they are placed on the long string in ascending numerical order, beginning on the foot spot and advancing toward the foot rail.

When balls on or near the foot spot or long string interfere with the spotting of balls, the balls to be spotted are placed on the long string as close as possible to the foot spot without moving the interfering balls. Spotted balls are to be *frozen* to such interfering balls, except when the cue ball is interfering; balls to be spotted against the cue ball are placed as close as possible without being frozen.

If there is insufficient room on the long string between the foot spot and the foot-rail cushion for balls that must be spotted, such balls are then placed on the extension of the long string in front of the foot spot (between the foot spot and the *center spot*), as near as possible to the foot spot and in the same numerical order as if they were spotted behind the foot spot (lowest numbered ball closest to the center of the table).

(Note: There are special spotting rules in the games of snooker, cowboy pocket billiards and bottle pocket billiards.)

26. JAWED BALLS. If two or more balls are locked between the *jaws* or sides of the pocket, with one or more suspended in air, the referee shall inspect the balls in position and then he shall visually (or physically if he desires) project each ball directly downward from its locked position; any ball that in his judgment would fall in the pocket if so moved directly downward is a pocketed ball, while any ball that would come to rest on the bed of the table is not pocketed. The balls are then placed according to the referee's assessment, and play continues according to specific game rules as if no locking or jawing of balls had occurred.

27. ADDITIONAL POCKETED BALLS. If a player completes a legal, scoring stroke on which an object ball or balls in addition to the intended, called, required or designated ball or balls also drop, such additional balls shall be counted, credited and scored in accord with the scoring rules for the particular game. (Note: The following games have rules which modify, restrict or negate Rule 26: bank pool, cowboy pocket billiards, cribbage, oneball, one pocket, poker pocket billiards, snooker and eight ball.)

28. NONPLAYER INTERFERENCE. If the balls are moved (or a player bumped such that play is directly affected) by a nonplayer during match, the balls shall be replaced as near as possible to their original positions immediately prior to the incident, and play shall resume with no penalty on the player affected. If the match is officiated, the referee shall replace the balls. This rule shall also apply to act-of-God interference, such as earthquake, hurricane, light fixture falling, power failure, etc. If the balls cannot be restored to

GENERAL RULES

49

their original positions, replay the game with the original player breaking.

29. BREAKING SUBSEQUENT RACKS. When *short rack games* are being competed in a format requiring sets or races, the winner of each game breaks the next. The following are common options that may be designated by tournament officials: players alternate break, loser breaks, player trailing in games score breaks the next game.

30. PLAY BY INNINGS. Unless individual game rules specify differently, players alternate turns (innings) at the table, with a player's inning ending when he either fails to legally pocket a ball, or fouls.

When an inning ends free of a foul, the incoming player accepts the table in position, unless individual game rules indicate otherwise.

31. OBJECT BALL FROZEN TO CUSHION OR CUE BALL. This rule applies to any shot where the cue ball's first contact with a ball is with one that is frozen to a cushion or to the cue ball itself. After the cue ball makes contact with the frozen object ball, the shot must result in either a ball being pocketed, or the cue ball contacting a cushion, or the frozen ball being caused to contact a cushion (not merely rebounding from the cushion it was frozen to), or another object ball being caused to contact a cushion with which it was not already in contact. Failure to satisfy one of these four requirements is a foul. (Note: 14.1 and other games specify additional requirements and applications of this rule; see specific game rules.)

32. PLAYING FROM BEHIND THE STRING. When a player has the cue ball in hand behind the string (in the kitchen), he must drive the cue ball to a point outside the kitchen before it contacts either a cushion or an object ball. Failure to do so is either a foul, or at opponent's option, offending player can be required to replay the shot with the balls restored to their positions prior to the shot, with no foul penalty imposed.

(Exception: If an object ball lies on or outside the head string, and is thus playable, but so close that the cue ball contacts it before the cue ball is out of the kitchen, the ball can be legally played.)

TOURNAMENT POCKET–BILLIARD GAMES

Eight Ball

Except when clearly contradicted by these additional rules, the general rules of pocket billiards apply.

1. TYPE OF GAME. The game is call shot and is played with a cue ball and fifteen object balls, numbered one thru fifteen. One player must pocket balls of the group numbered one thru seven (solid colors), while the other player has nine thru fifteen (stripes). The player pocketing his group first and then legally pocketing the eight ball, wins the game.

2. CALL SHOT (GENTLEMEN'S CALL). In gentlemen's call, obvious balls and pockets do not have to be indicated. It is the opponent's right to ask which ball and pocket if he is unsure of the shot. Banks and combinations are not considered obvious and both the object ball and the pocket must be called. When calling the shot, it is never necessary to indicate details such as the number of cushions, banks, kisses, caroms, etc. If the object ball is not legally pocketed and other object balls are pocketed, then the shooter's balls that were pocketed would be spotted and any of the opponent's balls remain pocketed; however if playing on a table designed for coin operation, all pocketed balls would remain pocketed. Note: any rule that requires the spotting of an illegally pocketed ball will only apply if the table is not designed for coin operated play.

3. THE RACK. The balls are racked in a triangle at the foot of the table with the eight ball in the center of the triangle, the first ball of the rack on the foot spot, a stripe ball in one corner of the rack and a solid ball in the other corner (figure 8–1).

4. ALTERNATING BREAK. Winner of coin toss has option to break. During individual competition, players will alternate breaking on each subsequent game.

5. LEGAL BREAK SHOT. (Defined) To execute a legal break, the breaker (with the cue ball behind the head string) must either pocket

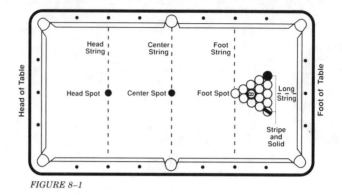

FIGURE 8–1

a ball or drive four numbered balls to the rail. If he fails to make a legal break, it is not a foul; however, the incoming player has the option of accepting the table in position and shooting, or having the balls re-racked and shooting the opening break himself. It is not necessary to hit the head ball (the ball that is on the foot spot) to initiate a legal break in eight ball.

6. SCRATCH ON A LEGAL BREAK. If a player *scratches* on a legal break shot, all balls pocketed are spotted including the eight ball, it is a foul, and the table is open. Note: Incoming player has cue ball in hand behind the head string and may not shoot an object ball that is behind the head string, unless he first shoots the cue ball past the head string and then by hitting a rail causes the cue ball to come back behind the head string and hit the object ball.

7. EIGHT BALL POCKETED ON THE BREAK. If the eight ball is pocketed on the break, the breaker may ask for a re-rack or have the eight ball spotted and continue shooting. If the breaker scratches while pocketing the eight ball on the break, the incoming player has the option of a re-rack or having the eight ball spotted and begin shooting with ball in hand behind the head string.

8. HEAD STRING RULE. This rule applies only when the opening player scratches on the break, and the incoming player has ball in hand behind the head string. The incoming player may place the cue ball anywhere behind the head string. If the player places the cue ball on or in front of the head string and shoots, it is a foul. He may shoot at any object ball as long as the base of the object ball (the point of the ball touching the table) is on or past the head string. He may not shoot at any ball the base of which is behind the head string, unless he first shoots the cue ball past the head string and then by hitting a rail causes the cue ball to come back behind the head string and hit the object ball. The base of the ball determines whether it is within or out of the head string. If the incoming player inadvertently places the cue ball in front of the head string, it is a good gesture for his opponent to inform him before he shoots to avoid confusion.

9. OPEN TABLE. (Defined) The table is open when the choice of groups (stripes or solids) has not been determined. When the table is open, it is legal to hit a solid first to make a stripe or vice versa. Note: The table is always open immediately after the break shot. When the table is open it is legal to hit any solid or stripe or the eight ball first in the process of pocketing the called stripe or solid. On an open table, all illegally pocketed balls are spotted.

10. CHOICE OF GROUP. The choice of stripes or solids is not determined on the break even if balls are made from one or both groups. The table is always open immediately after the break shot. The choice of group is only determined when a player legally pockets a called object ball after the break shot.

11. LEGAL SHOT. (Defined) On all shots (except on the break and when the table is open), the shooter must hit one of his group of balls first and pocket an object ball, or cause the cue ball or any object ball to contact a rail. Note: It is okay for the shooter to bank the cue ball off a rail before contacting his object ball; however, after contact with his object ball, an object ball must be pocketed, or the cue ball or any object ball must contact a rail.

12. SAFETY PLAY. Safety play is defined as a legal shot. If the shooting player intends to play safe by pocketing an obvious object ball, then prior to the shot, he must declare a safety to his opponent. If this is not done, the shooter will be required to shoot again. The shooter's object ball is considered illegally pocketed and must be spotted.

13. SCORING. A player is entitled to continue shooting until he fails to legally pocket a ball of his group. After a player has legally pocketed all of his group of balls, he shoots to pocket the eight ball.

14. FOULS. The following infractions result in fouls:
  a. Failure to execute a legal shot as defined above.
  b. A scratch shot (shooting the cue ball into a pocket or off the table).
  c. A scratch shot on a legal break.
  d. Shooting without at least one foot touching the floor.
  e. Moving or touching the cue ball in any fashion by means other than legal play.
  f. Shooting a jump shot over another ball by scooping the cue stick under the cue ball. A jump shot executed by striking the cue ball above center is legal. Note: A player does not commit a foul when he accidentally miscues and causes the cue ball to jump above the surface of the table.
  g. In organized competition (league or tournament play), if a team member advises or coaches another team member who is the shooter at the time, it is a foul on the team member shooting.

15. FOUL PENALTY. Opposing player gets cue ball in hand. This means that the player can place the cue ball anywhere on the table (does not have to be behind the head string except on opening break). This rule prevents a player from making intentional fouls which would put his opponent at a disadvantage. With cue ball in hand, the player may position the cue ball on the table by hand (more than once if necessary). After placing the cue ball, the shaft and ferrule of the cue stick (not the tip) may also be used for positioning the cue ball for shooting.

16. COMBINATION SHOTS. Combination shots are allowed. However, the eight ball cannot be used as a first ball in the combination except when the table is open.

17. ILLEGALLY POCKETED BALLS. An object ball is considered to be illegally pocketed when it is pocketed on the same shot a foul is committed, or the called ball did not go in the designated pocket, or a safety is called prior to the shot. If not on tables designed for coin-operated play, the shooter's illegally pocketed balls are spotted on the foot spot and opponent's balls remain pocketed. If playing on tables designed for coin-operated play, all illegally pocketed balls remain off the table.

18. SPOTTING BALLS. Whenever an object ball is to be spotted, the object ball is spotted on the long string as close to the foot spot as possible and shall be frozen to any interfering ball except the cue ball. The balls are spotted in numerical order starting with the lowest-numbered ball.

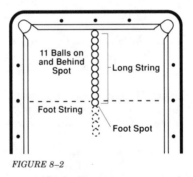

FIGURE 8–2

19. OBJECT BALLS JUMPED OFF THE TABLE. If any object ball is jumped off the table, it is a miss and loss of turn, not a foul, unless it is the eight ball, which is a loss of game. The shooter's object ball(s) is spotted and any of the opponent's jumped balls will be pocketed.

20. OBJECT BALL FROZEN TO CUSHION. This rule applies when the object ball to be struck by the cue ball is frozen to the rail. After the cue ball contacts the object ball you must pocket the frozen ball or any other object ball, or drive the frozen object ball to another cushion, or drive the cue ball or another object ball to any cushion. Failure to do so is a foul. When there is any doubt whether the object ball is frozen to a cushion, the player should ask for a ruling before shooting.

21. DOUBLE HIT. If the cue ball is touching your object ball prior to the shot, the player may shoot toward it with a level cue, providing that his cue stick strikes rather than pushes the cue ball. If the cue ball is close, but not frozen to the object ball, the cue must be elevated to a 45-degree angle when shooting in the general direction of the line of the two balls. A level cue may be used if aiming 45 degrees or more off the line of the two balls.

22. PLAYING THE EIGHT BALL. When shooting at the eight ball, a scratch or foul is not loss of game if the eight ball is not pocketed or jumped from the table. Incoming player has ball in hand.

23. LOSS OF GAME. A player loses the game if he commits any of the following infractions:

a. Fouls when pocketing the eight ball. (Exception: See eight ball pocketed on the break)

b. Pockets the eight ball on the same stroke as the last of his group of balls.

c. Jumps the eight ball off the table at any time.

d. Pockets the eight ball in a pocket other than the one designated.

e. Pockets the eight ball when it is not the legal object ball.

24. STALEMATED GAME. If in three consecutive turns at the table by each player (six turns total), they purposely foul or scratch and both players agree that attempting to pocket or move an object ball will result in immediate loss of game, then the game will be considered a stalemate. The balls will then be re-racked and the breaker of the stalemated game will break again. Note: Three consecutive fouls by one player is not a loss of game.

25. DISQUALIFICATION. The league or tournament director has the right to disqualify any player from competition and the player forfeits the right to prize money and/or any other awards for unsportsmanlike conduct or tactics detrimental to the league or tournament.

26. SPECTATOR COACHING. Spectators on the sidelines should not be allowed to advise or coach a player during competition. If after asking a spectator not to coach a player and he continues to do so, the referee should ask the spectator to leave the tournament area.

27. SHOOTING TIME RULE. If in the opinion of the referee a player is impeding the progress of the tournament or game with consistently slow play, the referee can warn the player and then at his discretion impose a one-minute time limit for that person between shots. If the referee does impose a one-minute time limit and that limit is exceeded, a foul will be called and the incoming player shall have ball in hand.

Nine Ball

(PROFESSIONAL RULES)

Rules provided by the Professional Billiard Tour Association, P.O. Box 5599, Spring Hill, Fl. 34608-3853

1. TYPE OF GAME.

Nine ball is played with nine object balls numbered one through nine and a cue ball. On each shot the first ball the cue ball contacts must be the lowest numbered ball on the table, but the balls need not be pocketed in order. If a player pockets any ball on a legal shot, he remains at the table for another shot, and continues until he misses, fouls, or wins the game by pocketing the nine ball. After a miss, the incoming player must shoot from the position left by the previous player, but after a foul the incoming player may start with the cue ball anywhere on the table. Certain serious fouls are penalized by loss of the game. Players are not required to call any shot. A match ends when one of the players has won the required number of games.

Detailed rules for nine ball are given below, followed by the definitions of some technical terms. These rules do not cover specifications of tables and balls, sanctioning conditions, or the handling of prize funds.

2. BEGINNING PLAY.

2.1 Order of Play. Order of play for the first game is determined by lag. The winner of the lag may break the first rack or assign the break to his opponent. In subsequent games of the match the winner of the previous game will break.

2.2 Racking the Balls. The object balls are racked in a diamond shape, with the one ball at the top of the diamond and on the foot spot, the nine ball in the center of the diamond, and the other balls in arbitrary order. If the one ball is not touching both of the adjacent balls, the breaker may ask the referee to re-rack the balls prior to the break. The cue ball begins in hand above the head string.

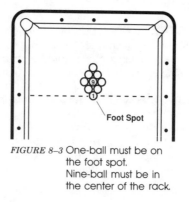

FIGURE 8–3 One-ball must be on the foot spot.
Nine-ball must be in the center of the rack.

2.3 Break Shot. The rules governing the break shot are the same as for other shots except:

a. If the cue ball is pocketed or driven off the table, and no other foul is committed, the incoming player has cue ball in hand above the head string. If the one ball is not below the head string, it is spotted on the long string. The incoming player may pass the shot after a scratch on the break, and the breaker must then shoot with ball in hand above the head string.

b. The breaker must attempt an open break—he must attempt to pocket a ball. Failure to do so is a standard foul.

c. If the breaker fails to contact the one ball, it is not considered a foul, the balls are re-racked (if necessary), and the breaker breaks again, starting from behind the head string.

d. On the shot immediately following a legal break, the shooter may play a "push out" (see section 9.10).

3. CONTINUING PLAY.

If the breaker pockets one or more balls on a legal break, he continues to shoot until he misses, fouls, or wins the game. If the player misses or fouls, the other player begins his inning and shoots until he misses, fouls, or wins. The game ends when the nine ball is pocketed on a legal shot, or the game is forfeited for a serious infraction of the rules.

4. STANDARD FOULS.

When a player commits a standard foul, he must relinquish his run at the table and all balls pocketed on the foul shot are spotted on the long string in numerical order. The incoming player is awarded ball in hand; prior to his first shot he may place the cue ball anywhere on the table. If a player fouls during the other player's inning, the shooter is awarded ball in hand, and if the foul had an effect on the position of the balls, the referee will restore the position if requested to do so by the shooter. If a player commits several standard fouls on one shot, they are counted as only one foul. The following are standard fouls:

4.1 Scratch. Pocketing the cue ball or driving it off the table is a foul.

4.2 Bad hit. If the first object ball contacted by the cue ball is not the lowest-numbered ball on the table, the shot is a foul.

4.3 No rail. If no object ball is pocketed, failure to drive the cue ball or some object ball to a rail after the cue ball contacts the object ball is a foul.

4.4 Foot. Failure to have at least one foot in contact with the floor at the moment the cue tip contacts the cue ball is a foul.

4.5 Moving ball. Shooting while any ball is moving or spinning is a foul.

4.6 Push shot. It is a foul if the cue ball is pushed by the cue tip, with contact being maintained for more than the momentary time commensurate with a stroked shot. If, in the referee's judgment, the player lays the cue tip against the cue ball and then pushes on into the shot, maintaining contact beyond the normal momentary split second, the stroke is a foul and must be so called.

4.7 Double hit. If the cue ball is touching the lowest-numbered ball prior to the shot, the player may shoot toward it, providing that his cue stick strikes rather than pushes the cue ball. When the cue ball and object ball are close to each other, and if during the stroke it cannot be determined if the cue tip leaves the cue ball before contact is made on the object ball, the cue ball must not maintain both a similar speed and a similar direction as the object ball or else it will be deemed a foul.

4.8 Touched object ball. It is a foul to touch a moving ball or to allow that ball to hit any foreign object, such as a cube of chalk. (The top of the rail is not considered to be a foreign object.) It is not a foul to accidentally touch stationary object balls while in the act of shooting. If such an accident occurs, the player should allow the referee to restore the object balls to their correct positions. If the player does not allow such a restoration, and a ball set in motion as a normal part of the shot touches such an unrestored ball, or passes partly into a region originally occupied by a disturbed ball, the shot is a foul. In short, if the accident has any effect on the outcome of the shot, it is a foul. In any case, the referee must restore the positions of the disturbed balls as soon as possible, but not during the shot. It is a foul to play another shot before the referee has restored any accidentally moved balls.

At the nonshooting player's option, the disturbed balls will be left in their new positions. In this case, the balls are considered restored, and subsequent contact on them is not a foul.

If the match is to be televised, touching a stationary ball is a foul. The incoming player still has the option of restoration.

4.9 Placement. Touching any object ball with the cue ball while it is in hand is a foul.

4.10 Object ball. Players may touch object balls only to assist the referee in his duties. If a player intentionally touches any object ball for any other purpose while a game is in progress, whether that object ball is in play or not, he has fouled. (This rule does not apply to the usual collisions between the balls.)

4.11 Cue ball. Except for ball-in-hand placement, if a player touches the cue ball with anything other than the chalked surface of his cue tip, he has fouled. The player may place the cue ball with anything other than the chalked surface of his cue tip.

4.12 Interference. If the nonshooting player distracts his opponent or interferes with his play, he has fouled. If a player shoots out of turn, or moves any ball except during his inning, it is considered to be interference.

4.13 Devices. Using any device in an uncustomary manner in lining up or executing a shot is a foul.

4.14 Practice. While a game is in progress, practice is not allowed. Taking a shot that is not part of that game is a foul.

5. SERIOUS FOULS.

The following serious fouls are penalized by the loss of one game, if the referee has warned the player before the foul. If the referee fails to warn the player, any foul is penalized like a standard foul, except as noted.

5.1 Three consecutive fouls. If a player fouls three times without making an intervening legal shot, he loses the game. The three fouls must occur in one game. The warning must be given between the second and third fouls.

5.2 Assistance. While a match is in progress, players are not allowed to ask spectators for assistance in planning or executing shots. If a player asks for and receives such assistance, he loses the game. Any spectator who spontaneously offers any significant help to a player will be removed from the area (see section 7.10).

5.3 Failure to leave the table. If a player does not stop shooting as soon as the referee has called a foul, he loses the game. The calling of the foul is considered to be the referee's warning to the player.

5.4 Slow play. If in the opinion of the referee a player is impeding the progress of the tournament or game with consistently slow play, the referee can warn the player and then at his discretion impose a one minute time limit for that person between shots. If the referee does impose a one minute time limit and that limit is exceeded, a foul will be called and the incoming player shall have cue ball in hand. Timing the first shot of a player's inning will begin ten seconds after the balls stop rolling from the previous player's turn.

5.5 Head string. After a scratch on a break shot, the cue ball is in hand above the head string. The referee should say, "Above the head string," when he hands the cue ball to the player, which constitutes the warning. If the player intentionally places the cue ball on or below the head string he loses the game. If the player accidentally places the cue ball slightly below the head string, the referee must warn him again, or no foul is considered to have occurred. With cue ball in hand above the head string, if the player plays directly on an object ball above the head string without the cue ball first crossing the head string, he loses the game. No warning is required in this last case.

5.6 Suspended play. If a player shoots while play is suspended by the referee, he loses the game. Announcement of the suspension is considered sufficient warning.

5.7 Concession. If a player concedes, he loses the game. The unscrewing of a jointed cue stick, except to replace a shaft, is considered to be a concession. No warning from the referee is required in the case of a concession.

6. OTHER SITUATIONS AND INTERPRETATIONS.

6.1 Outside interference. When outside interference occurs during a shot that has an effect on the outcome of that shot, the referee will restore the balls to the positions they had before the shot, and the shot will be replayed. If the interference had no effect on the shot, the referee will restore the disturbed balls and play will continue. If the balls cannot be restored to their original positions, the game will be replayed with the original player breaking.

6.2 Balls moving spontaneously. A ball may settle slightly after it appears to have stopped, possibly due to slight imperfections in the ball or the table. Unless this causes a ball to fall into a pocket, it is considered a normal hazard of play, and the ball will not be moved back. If a ball falls into a pocket as the result of such settling, it is replaced as close as possible to its original position. If a ball falls into a pocket during or just prior to a shot, and has an effect on the shot, the referee will restore the position and the shot will be replayed. Players are not penalized for shooting while a ball is settling.

6.3 Jump shots. It is legal to cause the cue ball to rise off the bed of the table by elevating the cue stick on the shot, and forcing the cue ball to rebound from the bed of the table (see section 4.11). Any miscue when executing a jump shot is a foul.

6.4 Illegal jump shot (i.e. scoop shots). If a player plays a shot with extreme draw with the intention of miscuing to make the cue ball jump over an object ball, he has fouled (see jump shots, section 6.3).

6.5 Protesting fouls. If a player thinks that the referee has failed to call a foul, he must protest to the referee before the next shot starts. If he fails to do so, and the foul goes unpenalized, the foul is considered not to have occurred. The referee is the final judge on matters of fact. If either player thinks that the referee is applying the rules incorrectly, and the dispute cannot be resolved by reference to the rule book, the referee must take the protest to the tournament director or his appointed substitute. The tournament director's decision on interpretation of the rules is final. A player may also protest if he thinks that the referee has called a foul incorrectly. In any case play is suspended until the protest is resolved.

6.6 Prompting warnings. When a player thinks that the referee is failing to issue a mandatory warning, he may remind the referee that such a warning is necessary.

6.7 Waiving specific rules. Prior to the start of tournament, the tournament director may choose to waive or modify specific rules, e.g., the loser of a game rather than the winner may break the following games.

6.8 Late start. A player must be ready to begin a match within fifteen minutes of the start of the match, or his opponent wins by forfeit. The starting time is considered to be the scheduled time or the time the match is announced, whichever is later.

6.9 Unsportsmanlike conduct. If the referee and the tournament director agree that a player is persistently behaving in a disruptive or unsportsmanlike manner, they may penalize him in any way they choose, including calling a foul on him, awarding the game or match to his opponent, or forfeiting all of his remaining matches.

7. INSTRUCTIONS FOR THE REFEREE.

The referee will maintain order and enforce these rules. He is the final judge in all matters of fact. His duties include but are not limited to the following:

7.1 Before the match. Before the match, the referee will clean the table and balls if necessary. He will ensure that chalk and mechanical bridges are available. He will mark the head string and long string with a pencil, if they are not already marked.

7.2 Racking. The referee will rack the balls as tightly as possible, which means each ball should be touching its neighbors. Tapping a ball into place is not recommended. It is preferable to thoroughly brush the area of the rack to even out the cloth.

7.3 Calling fouls. The referee will call fouls as soon as they occur and will inform the incoming player that he has ball in hand.

7.4 Clearing pockets. On tables that do not have ball-return systems, the referee will remove pocketed object balls from full or nearly full pockets. It is the player's responsibility to see that this duty is performed; he has no recourse if a ball rebounds from a full pocket.

7.5 Cleaning balls. During a game a player may ask the referee to clean one or more balls. The referee will clean any visibly soiled ball.

7.6 Soliciting information. If the referee does not have a clear view of a possible foul, he may ask spectators for assistance in determining what occurred. The referee will then weigh all evidence as he sees fit.

7.7 Warnings which are mandatory. The referee must warn a player who is about to commit a serious foul; otherwise any foul is considered to be a standard foul (except as specially noted). The referee must warn a player who has had two consecutive fouls; otherwise the player is considered to have had only one foul prior to the shot. The referee must warn a player when an object ball is touching a rail; otherwise any contact on that ball is considered to have driven it to that rail. The referee should issue warnings as soon as the corresponding situation arises. A warning given just as a shot starts is not considered sufficient; the player must be given enough time to react.

7.8 Restoring a position. When it becomes necessary, the referee will restore disturbed balls to their original positions to the best of his ability. The referee may ask for information for this purpose if he is not sure of the original positions. If the balls were disturbed by a player, the other player has the option of preventing the restoration. In the case, the referee should clearly indicate where the balls will be moved to if they are restored, and only restore the balls if requested to do so.

7.9 Advice and rules clarifications. The referee must not give advice to the players on points of play except to clarify the rules. When asked for such clarification, the referee will explain the applicable rules to the best of his ability, but any misstatement by the referee will not protect a player from enforcement of the actual rules. When asked, the referee must tell a player how many consecutive fouls have been committed, what the score is, whether the cue ball is touching an object ball, what the restored position would be, etc.

7.10 Suspending play. The referee has the authority to suspend play during protests by players and whenever he feels that conditions are unsuitable for play to continue. If a spectator is interfering with the game, play may be suspended until that spectator is removed from the area.

8. PLAYING WITHOUT A REFEREE.

When a referee is not available, the player who is not shooting will assume the duties of the referee.

8.1 Third opinion. When a shot comes up that seems likely to lead to controversy, the player not shooting should temporarily enlist a tournament official or a third party to judge the legality of the execution.

8.2 Resolving disputes. Any dispute between the two players will be resolved by the tournament director or his appointed substitute.

8.3 Split hit. If the cue ball strikes the lowest-numbered ball and another object ball at approximately the same instant, and it cannot be determined which ball was hit first, the judgment will go in favor of the shooter.

9. DEFINITIONS.

The following definitions apply throughout these rules.

9.1 Shot, inning, game, match. A shot begins at the instant the cue tip contacts the cue ball, and ends when all balls in play stop rolling and spinning (see section 9.3).

A player's innings begins when it is legal for him to take a shot and ends at the end of a shot on which he misses, fouls or wins, or when he fouls between shots.

A game starts when the referee has finished racking the balls, and ends at the end of a legal shot which pockets the nine or when a player forfeits the game as the result of a foul.

A match starts when the players are ready to lag and ends when the deciding game ends.

9.2 Behind the head string. A ball is behind the head string if its center is inside the head string (toward the head end of the table). A ball is outside the head string if its center is on or below the head string (toward the foot or rack end of the table).

9.3 Stopped. A ball resting on the brink of a pocket is considered to have stopped if it remains motionless for five seconds, as determined by the referee. If any player or spectator causes such a ball to fall into the pocket before the five-second limit by bumping or otherwise moving the table, the ball will be replaced at the edge of the pocket and is not considered pocketed. The time begins when all other balls have stopped and the shot ends at the end of the five seconds.

9.4 Pocketed. A ball is considered pocketed when it comes to rest in a pocket or enters the ball-return system of the table. A ball which hits the lining of the pocket or another ball already in the pocket and returns to the surface of the table or jumps off the table is not considered pocketed. If a ball comes to rest at the brink of a pocket so that it is partly supported by another ball, it is considered to be pocketed if the removal of the supporting ball would cause the supported ball to fall into the pocket.

9.5 To a rail. A ball is driven to a rail if it is not touching a rail, and then touches a rail. A ball which is touching a rail at the start of a shot and then is forced into the same rail is not considered to have been driven to that rail unless it leaves the rail and returns. A ball is considered to have been driven to a rail if it is driven off the table or touches the pocket back or facing.

9.6 Spotting balls. All object balls that have been pocketed illegally or driven off the table are spotted by the referee after the shot is over. Object balls are spotted by placing them on the long string, on or below the foot spot if possible, and as close to the foot spot as possible. If several balls are to be spotted at the same time, they are spotted in numerical order.

9.7 In hand. When the cue ball is in hand, the player may place the cue ball anywhere on the bed of table, except in contact with an object ball. He may continue to adjust the position of the cue ball until he takes a shot. With ball in hand above the head string (after a scratch on the break), the player may not place the cue ball below the head string.

9.8 Off the table. An unpocketed ball is considered to be driven off the table if it comes to rest other than on the bed of the table. It is not a foul to drive an object ball off the table. It is spotted and play continues.

9.9 Lag. Players lag by shooting at the same time from behind the head string to contact the foot rail and then have the cue ball come to rest as close as possible to the head rail. Object balls may be substituted if two cue balls are not available. A player loses the lag if his cue ball crosses the center line of the table, does not contact the foot rail, is pocketed or driven off the table, or hits any object ball. Ties are replayed. The distance of the cue ball to the head rail is the shortest distance between the cue ball and any cloth-covered part of the rail (the cushion nose or the pocket facing).

9.10 Push out. The player who shoots the shot immediately after a legal break may play a push out in an attempt to move the cue ball into a better position for the option that follows. On a push out, the cue ball is not required to contact any object ball or any rail, but all other foul rules still apply. The player must announce his intention of playing a push out before the shot, or the shot is considered to be a normal shot. Any ball pocketed on a push out does not count and is spotted. Following a legal push out, the incoming player is permitted to shoot from that position or to pass the shot back to the player who pushed out. A push out is not considered to be a foul as long as no rule (except 4.2 or 4.3) is violated. An illegal push out is penalized according to the type of foul committed.

14.1 Continuous

Except when clearly contradicted by these additional rules, the general rules of pocket billiards apply.

1. TYPE OF GAME. 14.1 continuous is generally considered to be the game that provides the greatest all-around test of complete pocket-billiard playing skill, requiring great concentration, accuracy, shot-making, defense, patience and knowledge. It is the only commonly played game in which a shooter can play a single inning through rack after rack of balls. Players may shoot at any ball on the table at any time, but they must call the ball and the pocket on each shot. Unending variety . . . and challenge!

2. PLAYERS. Two (or two teams).

3. BALLS USED. Standard set of object balls numbered one through fifteen plus cue ball.

4. THE RACK. Standard triangle rack with the front apex ball on the foot spot, one ball on the racker's right corner, five ball on left corner. Other balls placed at random.

5. OBJECT OF THE GAME. Score the predetermined point total for a game prior to the opponent (usually 150 in major-tournament play or any agreed upon total in casual play).

6. SCORING. Any ball legally pocketed counts one point for the shooter.

7. OPENING BREAK. Starting player must either designate a ball and a pocket into which that ball will be pocketed and accomplish the shot, or cause the cue ball to contact a ball and then a cushion, plus cause two object balls to contact a cushion. Failure to meet at least one of the above requirements is a breaking violation. Offender's score is assessed a two-point penalty for each breaking violation. In addition, the opponent has the choice of accepting the table in position, or having the balls reracked and requiring the offending player to repeat the opening break. That choice continues until the opening break is not a breaking violation, or until the opponent accepts the table in position. The three successive fouls rule does not apply to breaking violations.

If the starting player scratches on a legal opening break, he is charged with a foul and assessed a one point penalty, which applies toward the "Successive Fouls Penalties." The incoming player is awarded cue ball in hand behind the head string, with object balls in position.

8. RULES OF PLAY.

8.1 A legally pocketed ball entitles a shooter to continue at the table until he fails to legally pocket a called ball on a shot. A player may shoot any ball he chooses, but before he shoots, must designate the called ball and called pocket. He need not indicate any detail such as kisses, caroms, combinations, or cushions (all of which are legal). Any additionally pocketed ball(s) on a legal stroke is scored as one point for the shooter.

If a referee incorrectly calls a shot, a player should correct him before completing the shot. If a miscall does occur for any reason, the shot shall be credited if, in the referee's judgment, the player did legally execute the shot as intended.

8.2 On all shots, a player must cause the cue ball to contact an object ball and then pocket an object ball, or cause the cue ball or any object ball to contact a cushion. Failure to meet these requirements is a foul.

When an object ball is not frozen to a cushion, but is within a ball's width of a cushion (referee to determine by measurement if necessary), a player is permitted only two legal safeties on that ball using only the near rail. If such safety play is employed, that object ball is then considered frozen to the rail on the player's next inning. The general rules of pocket billiards' frozen-balls requirements apply if the player chooses to make his first cue ball contact with that object ball on his third shot.

(Note: If a player has committed a foul on his previous shot effort before playing this ball, he is allowed only one legal safety on the ball using the near rail. He must then meet the requirements of the frozen-ball rule on his next shot. If he has committed two consecutive fouls, he must immediately meet the requirements of the frozen-ball rule when playing this object ball. If such player fails to meet the requirements of the frozen-ball rule, he is considered to have committed a third successive foul and the appropriate point penalty is assessed as well as one point for each of the previous fouls. All fifteen balls are then re-racked and the player committing the infraction is required to break as at the beginning of the game.)

8.3 When the fourteenth ball of a rack is pocketed, play stops momentarily with the fifteenth ball remaining in position on the table; the fourteen pocketed balls are then racked (with the space at the foot spot vacant in the triangle). Player then continues, normally pocketing the fifteenth (or break ball) in such manner as to have the cue ball carom into the rack and spread the balls to facilitate the continuance of his run. However, player is not compelled to shoot the fifteenth ball; he may shoot any ball he desires.

See figure 8–4 if the fifteenth ball is pocketed on the same stroke as the fourteenth ball.

8.4 A player may call a safety rather than an object ball (for defensive purposes). Safety play is legal, but must comply with all applicable rules. Player's inning ends when a safety is played, and pocketed balls are not scored. Any object ball pocketed on a called safety is spotted.

8.5 A player may not catch, touch, or in any way interfere with a ball as it travels toward a pocket or the rack area on a shot (to include catching a ball as it enters a pocket by having a hand in the pocket). If he does, he is charged with a special "deliberate foul" and is penalized one point for the foul and an additional fifteen-point penalty, for a total of sixteen points. The incoming player then has the choice of accepting the table in position with the cue ball in hand behind the head string, or having all fifteen balls re-racked and requiring the offending player to shoot under the requirements of the opening break.

8.6 If the fifteenth (unpocketed) ball of a rack and/or the cue ball interferes with the triangle being lowered straight down into position for racking, refer to figure 8–4, which indicates the proper manner of relocating balls. (The lined-out boxes are those situations in which there is no interference; both balls remain in position.)

What to do if:

15th Ball Lies \ Cue Ball Lies	IN THE RACK	NOT IN THE RACK AND NOT ON HEAD SPOT*	ON HEAD SPOT*
IN THE RACK	15th Ball: foot spot. Cue Ball: in kitchen	15th Ball: head spot. Cue Ball: in position	15th Ball: center spot. Cue Ball: in position.
POCKETED	15th Ball: foot spot. Cue Ball: in kitchen.	15th Ball: foot spot. Cue Ball: in position	15th Ball: foot spot. Cue Ball: in position.
IN KITCHEN BUT NO ON HEAD SPOT*	15th Ball: in position. Cue Ball: head spot.	//////	//////
NOT IN KITCHEN & NOT IN THE RACK	15th Ball: in position. Cue Ball: in kitchen.	//////	//////
ON HEAD SPOT*	15th Ball: in position. Cue Ball: center spot.	//////	*On head spot means to interfere with spotting a ball on the head spot

FIGURE 8–4

8.7 When a player has the cue ball in hand behind the head string (as after a scratch) and all object balls are behind the head string, the object ball nearest the head string may be spotted at his request. If two or more balls are an equal distance from the head string, the

BILLIARDS

player may designate which of the equidistant balls he desires to have spotted.

9. ILLEGALLY POCKETED BALLS. All spotted, no penalty.

10. JUMPED OBJECT BALLS. All spotted after the balls come to rest. No penalty.

11. CUE BALL AFTER JUMPING OFF THE TABLE OR SCRATCH. Incoming player has cue ball in hand behind the head string, unless the provision of rule number two, or the "successive fouls penalties" (below) apply to the offender's foul and dictate alternate choices or procedures.

12. PENALTIES FOR FOULS. One point deducted for each foul; Note: more severe penalties for deliberate fouls (rule of play #5) and third "successive fouls" (below). Incoming player accepts cue ball in position unless foul was a jumped cue ball, pocket scratch, deliberate foul (rule #5) or third successive foul.

13. SUCCESSIVE FOUL PENALTIES. When a player commits a foul, he is penalized one point (or more as appropriate) and a notation is made and posted by the scorer that he is "on a foul." The player remains on a foul until his next shot attempt, at which time he may remove the foul by successfully pocketing a called ball, or completing a legal safety. If he fails to meet these requirements on his next turn at the table, he's penalized one point. The notation is changed to "on two fouls." If he fails to meet the requirements of successfully pocketing a called ball or completing a legal safety on his third consecutive turn at the table, a penalty of 20 percent of game total is assessed. For example: 100 point game, twenty balls; 150 point game, thirty balls.

The commission of a third successive foul automatically clears the offender's record of fouls.

All balls are then re-racked and the player committing the infraction is required to break as at the beginning of the game. Rules for the opening break apply.

It should be emphasized that successive fouls must be committed in successive turns (or playing attempts), not merely in successive innings. For example, if a player ends inning number six with a foul, steps to the table for inning number seven and fouls (now on two fouls), and then starts inning number eight with a legally pocketed ball before scratching on his second shot attempt of the inning, he has not committed three successive fouls, even though there were fouls in three successive innings. As soon as he legally pocketed the ball to start inning number eight, he cleared the two fouls. He is, of course, on one foul when he plays the first stroke attempt of inning number nine. Option: At the choice of the nonoffending player, the penalty for a third successive foul can be as follows: One point is deducted from the offender's score, and the cue ball is in hand for the nonoffender with the object balls in position. The offender's record is cleared of successive fouls as in the standard rules.

14. SCORING NOTE. The deduction of penalty points can result in negative scores. A running score can read "minus one," "minus two," "minus fifteen," etc. A player can win a game with a score of 150 while his opponent has scored but two fouls. The final score would read 150 to -2.

If a player fouls on a shot that has not pocketed a ball, the point penalty is deducted from his score at the end of the previous inning. If a player fouls and pockets a ball on the same shot, that ball is spotted (not scored) and the point penalty is deducted from his score at the end of the previous inning.

Seven Ball

Except when clearly contradicted by these additional rules, the general rules of pocket billiards apply.

TYPE OF GAME. Seven ball is a new, speedy rotational game designed to meet the time requirements of television. Averaging only about three minutes per game because contestants shoot at the same seven object balls, it permits players to show skills in making combination and carom shots, defensive shots and placement. At the same time, it is attractive to players of moderate skills, and readily adapts to handicapping by limiting the number of pockets in which the better contestant can legally pocket the game-winning seven ball. Any nationwide commercial use of this game (patent pending) should be cleared in advance with Big Fights, Inc., 9 East 40th St., New York, New York, 10016.

PLAYERS. Two (or two teams).

BALLS USED. Object balls numbered one through seven, plus cue ball.

THE RACK. A special circular rack has been designed for this game. A standard diamond rack (as used in nine ball) may also be used by turning it sideways.

The balls are racked in a circle on the foot spot, with the one ball at the apex (twelve o'clock) and the balls increasing numerically one through six (clockwise in a circle) with the seven ball in the middle of the circle (figure 8–5).

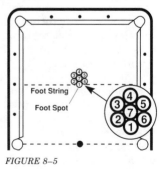

FIGURE 8–5

OBJECT OF THE GAME. To legally pocket the seven ball.

SCORING. The balls have no point value. The player legally pocketing the seven ball is credited with a game won.

OPENING BREAK. The starting player must make an open break, or legally pocket an object ball. If he fails to do so, incoming player has the choice of foul penalty #1 (see below), or having the balls re-racked and shooting the opening break shot himself. In subsequent games players alternate the break shot.

RULES OF PLAY.

1. A legal shot requires that the cue ball's first contact be with the lowest-numbered ball on the table. A player must then pocket a ball, or cause the cue ball or any object ball to contact a cushion. Failure to meet these requirements is a foul and foul penalty #2 applies (see below).

2. A legally pocketed ball entitles a shooter to remain at the table until he fails to pocket a ball on a legal shot.

3. After a legal opening break, opponent chooses which side of the table (any of the three pockets on one side) into which he will pocket the seven ball. Balls one through six may be pocketed on either side of the table.

4. Pocketing the seven ball on a fair opening break wins the game.

5. Any violation of general rules results in penalty #2.

LOSS OF GAME. A player loses the game if he commits any of the following infractions: (a) pockets the seven ball in a nonassigned pocket after the break; (b) scratches when the seven ball is his legal object ball; (c) pockets the seven ball on an illegal shot; (d) misses when the seven ball is his object ball (optional—an alternative is to assess foul penalty #2); (e) commits three successive fouls.

ILLEGALLY POCKETED OBJECT BALLS. All spotted, penalty #2 applies. (Optional for coin-operated tables: all balls remain pocketed; penalty #2 applies.)

JUMPED OBJECT BALLS. All spotted; no penalty.

CUE BALL AFTER JUMP OR SCRATCH. Incoming player has cue ball in hand.

PENALTY FOR FOULS. No point penalty. (1) Incoming player has cue ball in hand behind the head string and object balls in position, but if the lowest numbered object ball is also behind the head string, it must be spotted. (2) Cue ball in hand anywhere on the table.

VARIATION. Players of unequal ability may be handicapped by assigning them more or less pockets in which they can play the seven

·· POCKET-BILLIARD GAMES

(69)

ball. It is suggested that more skilled players shoot the seven ball into the side pocket on their side of the table. Players may also agree that the seven ball can be pocketed anywhere on the table.

Ten Ball

Except when clearly contradicted by these additional rules, the general rules of pocket billiards apply.

TYPE OF GAME. Ten ball is a variation of rotation in which a rack of just ten object balls is employed. As you will discern from the following rules, it is virtually the same game as nine ball, but with the extra ball adding both additional difficulty and generally fewer balls being pocketed on the opening break (particularly the ten, or game ball). Still, accomplished players turn it into a fast, action-packed game!

PLAYERS. Two or more, though two, three, or four is generally preferred.

BALLS USED. Object balls one through ten, plus cue ball.

THE RACK. Triangle rack truncated by removal of the rear row of balls (rows 1-2-3-4) with the one ball on the foot spot, and the ten ball in the center of the third row; other balls may be placed entirely at random.

OBJECT OF THE GAME. To legally pocket the ten ball.

SCORING. The balls have no point value. The player legally pocketing the ten ball is credited with a game won.

OPENING BREAK. The starting player must either make an open break, or legally pocket an object ball. If he fails to do so, incoming player has the choice of cue ball in hand behind the head string and object balls in position, or having the balls re-racked and shooting the opening break shot himself.

RULES OF PLAY

1. A legal shot requires that the cue ball's first contact with a ball is with the lowest numbered ball on the table, and then the player must either pocket a ball, or cause the cue ball or any object ball to contact a cushion. Failure to meet this requirement is a foul.

2. A legally pocketed ball entitles shooter to remain at the table until he fails to pocket a ball on a legal shot.

3. When a player legally pockets a ball, he must shoot again. He may not call a safety and spot a legally pocketed ball.

4. It is loss of game if a player commits three successive fouls.

ILLEGALLY POCKETED BALLS. All spotted; no penalty. (Common option, coin-operated play: None spotted except the game ball, no penalty.)

JUMPED OBJECT BALLS. All spotted; no penalty. (Common option, coin-operated play: None spotted except the game ball, no penalty.)

CUE BALL AFTER JUMPING OFF THE TABLE OR SCRATCH. Incoming player has cue ball in hand, except after the break shot.

PENALTY FOR FOULS. Incoming player is awarded cue ball in hand. (Note: rule #4 calls for loss of game if the foul is a third successive one.)

Rotation

Except when clearly contradicted by these additional rules, the general rules of pocket billiards apply.

TYPE OF GAME. Rotation requires that the cue ball must contact the lowest-numbered object ball first on each shot; any ball pocketed on a legal shot counts. It is not necessary to call balls or pockets. It is a formidable test of a player's imagination, shot-making and repertoire. Few games require more exacting position play.

PLAYERS. Two or more, though two-player games are generally preferred.

BALLS USED. Standard set of object balls one through fifteen plus cue ball.

THE RACK. Standard triangle rack with the one ball on the foot sot, two ball on the right rear corner, three ball on the left corner, and fifteen ball in the center. All other balls placed entirely at random.

OBJECT OF THE GAME. To score balls of greater total point value than opponent(s).

SCORING. Each legally pocketed object ball has a point value equal to its number. When a player's point total mathematically eliminates an opponent(s) from outscoring him (sixty-one points in a two-player game), the game is ended. If two or more players tie for highest point total after all fifteen object balls have been pocketed, the tied player who legally pocketed the last object ball is credited with an extra tie-breaking point and wins the game.

OPENING BREAK. The starting player must make an open break or legally pocket an object ball. If he fails to do so, the incoming player has the choice of shooting with cue ball in hand behind the head string and object balls in position or having the balls re-racked and shooting the opening break shot himself.

RULES OF PLAY.

1. A legal shot requires that the cue ball's first contact be with the lowest-numbered ball on the table. A player must then pocket a ball or cause the cue ball or any object ball to contact a cushion. Failure is a foul.

2. A legally pocketed ball entitles a shooter to remain at the table until he fails to pocket a ball on a legal shot. If necessary, a player is permitted only two legal safeties played by merely hitting that object ball (only) to the near cushion.

3. When a player legally pockets a ball, he must shoot again. He may not call a safety and spot a legally pocketed object ball.

4. When a player has the cue ball in hand behind the head string (as after a scratch) and the legal object ball is also behind the head string, the object ball may be spotted on the foot spot at his request.

5. It is a loss of game if a player commits three successive fouls. In more than a two-player game, balls pocketed by disqualified players remain off the table.

ILLEGALLY POCKETED BALLS.   All spotted.

JUMPED OBJECT BALLS.   All spotted; no penalty.

CUE BALL AFTER JUMPING OFF THE TABLE OR SCRATCH. Incoming player has cue ball in hand behind the head string.

PENALTY FOR FOULS.   No point penalty. Incoming player has the option of accepting the balls in position, or requiring offending player to shoot again with the table in position (if cue ball is in hand behind the head string, it is so for either player). Rule #5 takes precedence in the case of a third consecutive foul.

Bank Pool

Except when clearly contradicted by these additional rules, the general rules of pocket billiards apply.

TYPE OF GAME.   In bank pool, each shot must be a bank of an object ball into at least one cushion before the ball is pocketed. Straight-in shots are not legal. Is is by definition a demanding game, and fascinating to observe, particularly when the players are accomplished at the art of banking.

PLAYERS.   Two, three, four or five players, though two players are generally preferred.

BALLS USED.   Standard set of object balls one through fifteen, plus cue ball.

THE RACK.   Standard triangle rack; balls placed entirely at random.

OBJECT OF THE GAME. To score a greater number of balls than opponent(s).

SCORING. Each legally pocketed object ball is scored as one ball. In two-player games, the first player to score eight balls wins. In three-player games, the first player to score five balls wins. In four-player games, the first player to score four balls wins. In five-player games, the first scored ball (though credited to the shooter) is immediately spotted and the player continues to shoot; the first player to score four balls wins.

OPENING BREAK. Starting player must make an open break. If he fails to do so, incoming player has the choice of accepting the table in position and shooting, or having the balls re-racked and shooting the opening break shot himself. No balls may be scored on the opening break. If any balls are pocketed on a legal opening break shot, they are spotted and the breaker continues shooting.

RULES OF PLAY.

1. A legally pocketed ball entitles shooter to remain at the table until he fails to legally pocket a ball. Player may shoot any object ball, but must designate which ball, pocket and the cushion(s) that ball will contact. A legally pocketed ball must be driven into at least one cushion and rebounded into the called pocket.

2. A legally pocketed ball must be cleanly banked (i.e., no kisses, no combinations, or caroms involving the object ball are permitted). The cue ball may contact the object ball only once on a stroke.

3. On a legal scoring stroke, only the object ball is credited to the shooter. Any other balls pocketed on the same stroke do not count for the shooter, and may be subject to special spotting provisions regarding illegally pocketed balls.

4. When a player has the cue ball in hand behind the head string (as after a scratch) and all object balls are also behind the head string, the object ball nearest the head string may be spotted on the foot spot at his request. If two or more balls are an equal distance from the head string, the player may also designate which of the balls he desires to be spotted.

5. Cushion impact shall mean clear and distinct contact with a cushion by the object ball. Incidental contact with a cushion as the object ball approaches the called pocket shall not be considered an extra cushion(s) that would otherwise disqualify a legal shot. Rebounding of the object ball in the jaws of the pocket before dropping shall not be considered extra cushions unless otherwise designated by the player.

6. It is a loss of game if a player commits three successive fouls.

ILLEGALLY POCKETED BALLS. All spotted; no penalty. Special spotting rule: When in the course of a legal scoring stroke, an additional ball(s) is pocketed (or jumped off the table), spotting of the ball(s) is delayed until the shooter's inning ends. Should a player score the last ball on the table while any legally pocketed or jumped balls are being held for delayed spotting, those balls are then spotted so the player may continue his inning.

JUMPED OBJECT BALLS. All spotted; no penalty. Special spotting rule for illegally pocketed balls may also apply to jumped object balls.

CUE BALL AFTER JUMPING OFF THE TABLE OR SCRATCH. Incoming player has cue ball in hand behind the head string.

PENALTY FOR FOULS. The player committing the foul must spot one of his previously scored object balls for each foul committed. If a player fouls when he has no previously pocketed balls to spot up, he "owes" for such fouls, and must spot balls after each scoring inning until his owed fouls are eliminated. After fouls other than jumped cue ball or cue-ball scratch, incoming player accepts the cue ball in position.

COMMON OPTION. In a simplified version of bank pool, players must designate only the ball and pocket (not the cushion order). Banks need not be clean. Removing the cushion designation portions of rule of #1, along with all of rule #2, makes the above rules fully applicable to the simplified version of bank pool.

One Pocket

Except when clearly contradicted by these additional rules, the general rules of pocket billiards apply.

TYPE OF GAME. One pocket is a unique game in which only two of the six pockets are employed for legal scoring. Any ball may be played and need not be called. What is required is that an object ball falls in the player's "target" pocket. It requires a wide variety of strokes, cue-ball control, shot-making ability, patience and defensive strategy.

PLAYERS. Two, or two teams.

BALLS USED. Standard set of object balls one through fifteen, plus cue ball.

THE RACK. Standard triangle rack; balls placed entirely at random.

OBJECT OF THE GAME. To score a total of eight object balls in a player's target pocket before opponent.

SELECTION OF POCKETS. Prior to the opening break shot, starting player chooses one of the corner pockets on the foot end of the table as his target pocket; opponent then has the other foot-end corner as his target pocket.

SCORING. A legally pocketed ball is scored as one ball for shooter. Any ball pocketed in opponent's target pocket counts, unless the cue ball should scratch on the same shot. If the shot constitutes a foul other than a scratch, the opponent is allowed to keep the ball. Shooter's inning ends on a scratch or foul and any balls pocketed in shooter's pocket do not count on a foul or scratch. In addition, the shooter is penalized one ball for a foul or scratch.

OPENING BREAK. Starting player must legally pocket an object ball into his targeted pocket or cause the cue ball to contact an object ball, and after contact at least one object ball must contact a cushion. Failure to do so is a foul. Note: Cue ball does not have to strike a rail on the opening break.

RULES OF PLAY

1. A legal shot requires that the cue ball contact an object ball and then pocket an object ball or cause the cue ball or an object ball to contact a cushion. Failure to do so is a foul.

2. A legally pocketed ball in a target pocket entitles the shooter to remain at the table until he fails to pocket a ball in his target pocket on a legal shot. Player may shoot any object ball he chooses, and any ball pocketed in his target pocket on an otherwise legal stroke is a scored ball.

3. Balls pocketed in the four nontarget pockets are illegally pocketed balls.

4. Balls pocketed by shooter in his opponent's target pocket are scored for the opponent, even if the stroke was a foul, but do not count if the cue ball scratches or jumps the table. However, if the stroke is not a foul and the shooter pockets a ball(s) in both target pockets, shooter's inning continues, with all legally pocketed balls scored to the appropriate player. If a shooter pockets a ball that brings the opponent's score to the number the opponent needed to win the game, the shooter has lost.

5. When a player has the cue ball in hand behind the head string (as after a scratch) and all object balls are also behind the head string, the object ball nearest the head string may be spotted at his request. If two or more balls are an equal distance from the head string, the highest-numbered ball is spotted.

6. Three successive fouls by the same player is loss of game.

ILLEGALLY POCKETED BALLS. All spotted. Special spotting rules: When a ball(s) is pocketed in a nontarget pocket (or jumped off the table), spotting is delayed until the shooter's inning ends. Should a player legally score the last ball(s) on the table while illegally pocketed (or jumped) ball(s) are being held for delayed spotting, those balls are then spotted so the player may continue his inning.

JUMPED OBJECT BALLS.   All spotted; no penalty.

CUE BALL AFTER JUMPING OFF THE TABLE OR SCRATCH. Incoming player has cue ball in hand behind the head string.

PENALTY FOR FOULS.   The player committing the foul must spot one of his previously scored object balls for each foul committed. If a player who fouls has no previously pocketed balls to spot up, he "owes" for such fouls, and must spot balls after each scoring inning until his owed fouls are eliminated. After fouls other than jumped cue ball or cue-ball scratch, incoming player accepts the cue ball in position.

THREE-FOUL PENALTY.   If a player scratches or fouls three consecutive turns at the table, it is a loss of game.

BREAKING SUBSEQUENT RACKS.   If a "race" or set of games is being played as a match, players alternate the break shot in subsequent games.

OTHER POPULAR POCKET-BILLIARD GAMES

Basic Pocket Billiards

Except when clearly contradicted by these additional rules, the general rules of pocket billiards apply.

TYPE OF GAME. The game of basic pocket billiards is a combination of the call-shot aspects of 14.1 continuous and the "anything goes" character of fifteen ball. It is a game well-suited for "mixed" (beginners and accomplished players) play, particularly in a team mode.

PLAYERS. Two, or two teams.

BALLS USED. Standard set of object balls one through fifteen, plus cue ball.

THE RACK. Standard triangle rack; balls placed entirely at random.

OBJECT OF THE GAME. To score eight balls before opponent.

SCORING. Any legally pocketed ball is scored as one ball.

OPENING BREAK. Starting player must legally pocket an object ball into his targeted pocket or cause the cue ball to contact an object ball, and after contact at least one object ball must contact a cushion. Failure to do so is a foul. Note: Cue ball does not have to strike a rail on the opening break.

Failure is a breaking violation; opponent can accept the table in position and shoot, or require that the balls be re-racked and offending player repeat the opening break until the requirements are satisfied.

If starting player pockets a ball on the opening break, it is a legally pocketed ball if no foul or other violation is committed, and he continues at the table. On all subsequent shots, however, he must comply with all the rules of play below.

RULES OF PLAY

1. A legally pocketed ball entitles shooter to continue at the table until he fails to pocket a ball on a legal shot. Player may shoot any ball he chooses, but before he shoots must designate a single ball that he will pocket; he need not indicate into which pocket the ball will score, kisses, caroms, combinations or cushions (all of which are legal).

2. On all shots subsequent to the opening break, player must cause the cue ball to contact an object ball, and then pocket an object ball, or cause an object ball or the cue ball to contact a cushion. Failure to do so is a foul.

3. When a player has the cue ball in hand behind the head string and all remaining object balls are behind the head string as well, the object ball nearest the head string may be spotted on the footspot at his request. If two or more balls are an equal distance from the head string, the player may designate which of the equidistant balls he desires to be spotted.

ILLEGALLY POCKETED BALLS. All spotted; no penalty.

OBJECT BALLS JUMPED OFF THE TABLE. All spotted; no penalty.

CUE BALL AFTER JUMPING OFF THE TABLE OR SCRATCH. Incoming player has cue ball in hand behind the head string.

PENALTY FOR FOULS. One scored ball is returned to the table (spotted) by fouling player for each foul committed. If player who fouls has no previously pocketed balls to spot up, he "owes" for such fouls, and must spot balls after each scoring inning until his owed fouls are eliminated. After fouls other than cue-ball jump or cue-ball scratch, incoming player accepts the cue ball in position.

Bottle Pool

Except when clearly contradicted by these additional rules, the general rules of pocket billiards apply.

TYPE OF GAME. A truly unique pocket-billiard game, bottle pool requires the use of an inexpensive but specially shaped and balanced leather or plastic container ("bottle" or "shaker bottle"), shaped much like some disposable beverage bottles. The play of bottle pool combines the ball-pocketing abilities of pocket billiards with the carom-making requirements of carom games.

PLAYERS. Two or more.

BALLS USED. Object balls one and two, plus cue ball.

THE RACK. No triangle needed; at the start of the game, the one

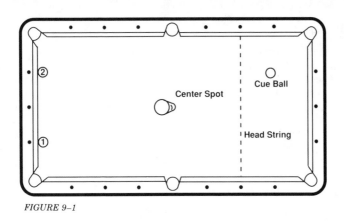

FIGURE 9–1

ball is frozen to the foot cushion, centered on the first diamond in from the racker's right corner pocket; the two ball is frozen to the foot cushion, centered on the first diamond in from the racker's left corner pocket; the bottle is placed open-end down on the center spot. (fig. 9–1).

OBJECT OF THE GAME. To score exactly thirty-one points prior to opponent(s).

SCORING. There are five scoring possibilities. A player executing a legal stroke scores as follows:

1. Pocketing the one ball: one point.

2. Pocketing the two ball: two points.

3. Carom of the cue ball on the two object balls: one point.

4. Carom of the cue ball from an object ball(s) to the bottle which knocks the bottle onto its side: five points.

5. Carom of the cue ball from an object ball(s) to the bottle which stands the bottle onto its base: automatic win of the game.

Should a player accomplish more than one scoring possibility on a shot, he scores for each; a single shot can result in a total of nine points scored.

Since exactly thirty-one points must be scored for victory (unless #5 above applies), a player must not exceed thirty-one; if he does, his inning ends and his score becomes only the total by which he exceeded thirty-one.

OPENING BREAK. No break shot as such. Beginning with cue ball in hand behind the head string, starting player must cause the cue ball to contact either the one ball or the two ball. If he fails to do so, incoming player can require that offending player repeat the opening shot until that requirement is satisfied.

RULES OF PLAY.

1. A legally executed scoring stroke entitles shooter to continue at the table until he fails to legally score on a shot, exceeds thirty-one points on a shot, causes an object ball to contact the bottle before the cue ball contacts the bottle (the entire shot is invalid and inning ends), or causes the bottle to be forced off the table or into a pocket (the entire shot is invalid and inning ends).

2. On all shots, player must cause the cue ball to contact an object ball. Failure to do so is a foul.

3. Cue ball must contact an object ball before it contacts the bottle. Failure to comply is a foul.

4. If player causes the bottle to be upset or upended by an object ball, the shot is a foul.

5. Player loses the game if he fouls in each of three consecutive innings at the table.

REPLACING UPSET BOTTLE. Whenever the bottle is upset, it is replaced on the table, open-end down, with the open end as close as possible to its position when the bottle came to rest. It is, of course, replaced prior to the next shot.

When the bottle is forced off the table or into a pocket (or into such position that the open end is over the pocket opening, making replacement as in the preceding paragraph impossible), the bottle is replaced on the center spot. If occupied, the head spot; if occupied, the foot spot; if occupied, hold out until center spot is vacant.

ILLEGALLY POCKETED BALLS. All spotted; no penalty (see special spotting rules below).

JUMPED OBJECT BALLS. All spotted; no penalty (see special spotting rules below).

SPECIAL SPOTTING RULES. After each shot is completed, any pocketed object balls are spotted prior to the next shot. They are spotted in the positions as at the start of the game. If a ball or the bottle prevents the free placement of an object ball to be spotted, the object ball is spotted on the center spot; if that is also occupied, the object ball is then spotted on the head spot. If both object balls are being spotted, follow the above, first spotting the one ball, then the two ball.

CUE BALL AFTER JUMPING OFF THE TABLE OR SCRATCH. Incoming player has cue ball in hand behind the head string.

PENALTY FOR FOULS. One point is deducted from offender's score for each foul. After fouls other than cue-ball jump or cue-ball scratch, incoming player accepts the cue ball in position.

Bowlliards

Except when clearly contradicted by these additional rules, the general rules of pocket billiards apply.

TYPE OF GAME. Bowlliards is a game that applies the scoring concepts of bowling to pocket billiards. It is one of the few games that can be quite interesting as a solitary exercise since, like bowling, there is a perfect game score to strive toward, and a player can measure his improvement quite easily over the course of time playing bowlliards.

PLAYERS. Any number.

BALLS USED. Any ten object balls, plus cue ball.

THE RACK. Standard triangle position (front apex ball on foot spot), using a 1-2-3-4 rack configuration.

OBJECT OF THE GAME. To score a perfect score of 300 points in ten frames (innings) in solitary play. In competition, to score a higher point total in ten innings than opponent(s).

SCORING. Each legally pocketed ball is scored as one point, regardless of ball number. The points scored as per the rules of play below are treated exactly as is the pinfall in bowling.

OPENING BREAK. At the start of player's inning (frame), he has a free break (no special balls-to-cushion or other requirements once break stroke commences, and a jumped or scratched cue ball is without penalty). Any balls pocketed on the break are spotted, and player then follows his break by beginning scoring play with object balls in position and cue ball in hand behind the head string. (The opening break takes place at the start of every inning.)

RULES OF PLAY.

1. A legally pocketed ball entitles shooter to continue at the table until he fails to pocket a called ball on a shot, or until he has scored the maximum total per inning possible (ten). Player may shoot any ball he chooses, but before he shoots, must designate a single ball that he will pocket and the pocket into which the ball will score; he need not indicate kisses, caroms, combinations or cushions (none of which are illegal).

2. Player has two chances to pocket the ten possible balls of each frame. If player legally pockets ten consecutive balls on his first chance of a frame, that frame is completed and player scores the frame exactly as a strike in bowling. If player fails to pocket ten consecutive balls on his first chance, he takes his second chance immediately. If he succeeds in legally pocketing the remaining balls of the ten on his second chance, the frame is completed and player scores it exactly as a spare in bowling. If player fails to legally pocket all ten balls in two chances, the frame is then completed and is scored just as in bowling. A "strike" in the tenth inning earns two extra shots, a spare one extra shot.

3. If players ties for high game total in competition, additional extra innings are played alternately by the tied players, with the first player posting a superior score to that of his opponent(s) being the winner (sudden death).

ILLEGALLY POCKETED BALLS. On the break, illegally pocketed balls are spotted prior to player beginning his scoring play (first chance of the frame). During scoring play, illegally pocketed balls are spotted.

JUMPED OBJECT BALLS. All spotted; no penalty.

CUE BALL AFTER JUMPING OFF THE TABLE OR SCRATCH. Only applies if occuring as player's first foul of a frame; player has cue ball in hand behind the head string to begin his second chance of the frame.

PENALTY FOR FOULS. One point is deducted from offender's score for each foul. If foul ends player's first chance of a frame, he has cue ball in hand behind the head string to begin his second chance of the frame.

Bumper Pool®

Rules and Regulations (Reprinted with permission of The Valley Company, Bay City, Michigan)

1. Bumper Pool® is played by two players or by four as partners.

2. Each side has five red balls or five white balls, one of each color being a marked cue ball.

3. To set up Bumper Pool®, place two red balls on each side of white cup (pocket) on markers, placing marked red ball directly in front of white cup. Place white balls in same position around the red cup (pocket).

4. Both players shoot their marked ball at the same time, hitting first the side cushion, banking the ball into or near his color cup. The player who plays his ball into or nearest his cup shoots again. Marked cue balls must be pocketed first. If a player sinks another ball before his marked ball is pocketed, his opponent may remove two of his own balls and drop them into his cup. In the event that both marked balls are pocketed on first shots, each player takes one of his remaining balls and spots it in front of his cup and both shoot at the same time, just as they did with the marked balls. From there on they take turns beginning with the player who pockets his ball or is nearest to his cup.

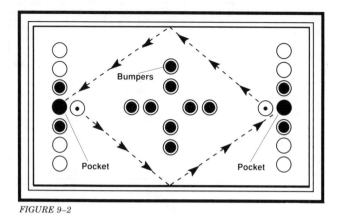

FIGURE 9–2

5. A player receives another shot upon sinking his own color ball in his own color cup.

6. In the event that a player causes a ball to leave the table, his opponent may place this ball anywhere he wishes, and in addition can remove two of his own balls and drop them into his cup as an additional bonus.

7. If a player sinks one of his opponent's balls there is no penalty, but if he sinks one of his own balls into his opponent's cup, or shoots one of his opponent's balls, his opponent may then drop two of his own balls into his cup.

8. No player is allowed to jump his ball over balls or bumpers in making shots. Penalty for this will be the same as in rule number 7.

9. The first player or team to sink all five of their balls is the winner, excepting that player forfeits game if he shoots his last ball into his opponent's cup.

10. The length of time that the winners may continue playing is governed by house rule.

Cowboy

Except when clearly contradicted by these additional rules, the general rules of pocket billiards apply.

TYPE OF GAME. Cowboy is another game that combines carom- and pocket-billiards skill, and employs a very unusual set of rules. Certainly a change of pace game; how many games have you played in which the cue ball must be pocketed on a carom of the one ball on the last shot??!

PLAYERS. Any number.

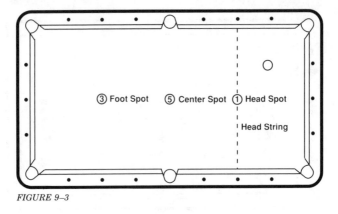

FIGURE 9–3

BALLS USED.   Object balls one, three and five, plus the cue ball.

THE RACK.   No triangle needed; the one ball is placed on the head spot, the three ball on the foot spot, and the five ball on the center spot.

OBJECT OF THE GAME.   To score 101 points prior to opponent(s).

SCORING.   The first ninety points exactly may be scored by any of these means on legal scoring strokes:

1.   Pocketing any of the object balls: points equal to the balls' numbers; and/or

2.   Carom of the cue ball off two of the object balls: one point; and/or

3.   Carom of the cue ball off the three object balls: two points.

Points ninety-one through 100 (exactly) must, and may only, be scored by execution of carom shots number 2 and number 3 above.

Point 101 (winning point) must be scored by caroming the cues all off the one ball into a called pocket without the cue ball contacting any other object ball.

Should a player accomplish more than one scoring possibility permitted by these rules, he scores for each; thus a single shot can result in a total of eleven points scored.

OPENING BREAK.   No break shot as such. Beginning with cue ball in hand behind the head string, starting player must cause the cue ball to contact the three ball first. If starting player fails to do so, incoming player has choice of requiring starting player to repeat the opening shot, or executing the opening shot himself.

RULES OF PLAY

1. A legally executed shot, conforming to the requirements of scoring (above), entitles shooter to continue at the table until he fails to legally execute and score on a shot.

2. On all shots, player must cause the cue ball to contact an object ball, and then the cue ball or object ball must contact a cushion. Failure to do so is a foul.

3. At the completion of each shot, any pocketed object balls are spotted on their same positions as at the start of the game. If the appropriate position is occupied, the ball(s) in question remain off the table until the correct position is vacant after a shot. If, however, the one ball would be held out as a player with exactly 100 points is to shoot, the balls are all placed as at the start of the game, and the player shoots with cue ball in hand behind the head string.

4. When a player scores his ninetieth point, the shot must score the number of points exactly needed to reach ninety; if the shot producing the ninetieth point also scores a point(s) in excess of ninety for the player, the shot is a foul.

5. When a player is playing for points ninety-one through 100 (which must all be scored on caroms solely), it is a foul to pocket an object ball on a shot.

6. When a player is playing for his 101st point, it is a foul if the cue ball is pocketed in a pocket other than the one called, or if the cue ball fails to contact the one ball, or if the cue ball contacts any other object ball.

7. When a player pockets the cue ball on an otherwise legal shot, and according to the special requirements given under scoring (above) for counting the 101st point, pocketing the cue ball on such a shot on the 101st point is not a foul.

8. Player loses the game if he fouls in each of three consecutive plays at the table.

ILLEGALLY POCKETED BALLS. All spotted per the provision of rules of play #3 (above), with no penalty, except in the special cases covered by the rules of play #4 and #5.

JUMPED OBJECT BALLS. All spotted; no penalty.

CUE BALL AFTER JUMPING OFF THE TABLE OR SCRATCH. Incoming player has cue ball in hand behind the head string.

PENALTY FOR FOULS. No point deduction, but any points scored on previous shots of the inning are not scored, and player's inning ends. After fouls other than cue-ball jump or cue-ball scratch, incoming player accepts the cue ball in position.

Cribbage

Except when clearly contradicted by these additional rules, the general rules of pocket billiards apply.

Type of Game. Cribbage pocket billiards derives its name from the fact that a score can only be made (with two exceptions) by pocketing a pair of balls in succession that add up to fifteen; a similarity exists with the popular card game of cribbage. In a sense, it represents a combination of a call-shot game and a set-order game, and is a bit different and quite interesting to play.

PLAYERS. Two.

BALLS USED. Standard set of object balls one through fifteen plus cue ball.

THE RACK. Standard triangle rack, with the fifteen ball in the center; with the exception that no two of the three corner balls should add up to a total of fifteen points, all other balls may be placed entirely at random.

OBJECT OF THE GAME. To score five points (cribbages) out of a possible total of eight.

DEFINITION OF A CRIBBAGE. A cribbage is a pair of object balls, legally pocketed, numerically totaling fifteen. There are just these seven regular cribbages: 1–14, 2–13, 3–12, 4–11, 5–10, 6–9 and 7–8. No other ball combinations can be cribbages except that when all seven regular cribbages have been legally pocketed, the fifteen ball becomes a legal cribbage by itself.

SCORING. Each legally pocketed cribbage counts one point for scoring player.

OPENING BREAK. Starting player must attempt an open break. Failure to do so is a breaking violation; opponent has the choice of requiring offending player to repeat the opening break (until requirements are satisfied), or playing the opening break shot himself.

Starting player is not required to call his shot; if any balls are pocketed on the break shot, they accrue to him and he may continue at the table.

RULES OF PLAY

1. To legally pocket a cribbage, the two balls must be pocketed in the same inning. When a player has legally pocketed a single ball on a shot, he must legally pocket the appropriate companion ball on his next shot, or it is a foul.

2. If a player scores a legal cribbage, he can continue his inning and attempt to score more cribbages in the same inning.

3. When not "on a cribbage," if a player pockets two or more balls on a shot that do not constitute a cribbage, he may next pocket any of the proper companion balls as he chooses, but must successively pocket each of those companion balls if he is to continue at the table. If he fails, it is a foul. If, while satisfying the requirements of scoring companion balls, other ball(s) are incidentally pocketed, they likewise accrue to him; he must continue to complete one of the cribbages he is "on" on each successive stroke (though in no special order). Failure to do so is a foul; all balls of uncompleted cribbages are spotted.

4. When a ball is pocketed legally, but player fails to complete the cribbage legally during the same inning, the ball is spotted.

5. On all shots, player must cause the cue ball to contact an object ball and then either pocket an object ball, or cause an object ball or the cue ball to contact a cushion. Failure to do so is a foul.

6. Player loses the game if he commits three successive fouls.

7. If the fifteen ball is pocketed before all the other cribbages have been legally pocketed, it is an illegally pocketed ball and is spotted immediately following the stroke (not inning) on which it was pocketed. No penalty.

8. When a player has the cue ball in hand behind the head string (as after a scratch) and all the object balls are also behind the head string, the object ball nearest the head string may be spotted on the foot spot at his request. If two or more balls are an equal distance from the head string, the player may also designate which of the equidistant balls he desires to be spotted.

ILLEGALLY POCKETED BALLS. All spotted; no penalty.

JUMPED OBJECT BALLS. All spotted; no penalty.

CUE BALL AFTER JUMPING OFF THE TABLE OR SCRATCH. Incoming player has cue ball in hand behind the head string.

PENALTY FOR FOULS Inning ends; no point or ball penalty (except per rule of play #6 above). Incoming player has the option of accepting the table in position and shooting, or shooting with cue ball in hand behind the head string.

Cutthroat

Except when clearly contradicted by these additional rules, the general rules of pocket billiards apply.

TYPE OF GAME. Cutthroat (also known as elimination) is a very popular game in social situations, rather than for serious competitive play. It is very enjoyable to play, fast and with simple rules.

A perfect game when there are an odd number of participants available.

PLAYERS. Three or five.

BALLS USED. Standard set of object balls one through fifteen plus cue ball.

THE RACK. Standard triangle rack with the first ball on the foot spot, and the six and eleven balls on the two corners; all other balls placed at random.

DETERMINATION OF GROUPS. In three-player game, starting player has the group of balls 1–5; second player has balls 6–10; third player has balls 11–15. In five-player game, starting player 1–3; second player 4–6; third 7–9; fourth 10–12; and fifth 13–15.

OBJECT OF THE GAME. To legally pocket your opponents' balls before the opponents legally pocket your group of balls.

SCORING. Group balls have no point value. The player with a ball(s) still on the table, when all the other groups' balls are legally pocketed, wins the game.

OPENING BREAK. Starting player must make an open break. If he fails to do so, incoming player may either accept the table in position and shoot or require that the balls be re-racked and shoot the opening break himself. All balls pocketed on a legal break remain pocketed.

RULES OF PLAY.

1. Players must decide prior to the game whether they are playing call shot or not.

2. A legal shot requires that the cue ball's first contact be with an opponent's object ball. On all shots, player must cause the cue ball to contact an object ball and then either pocket an object ball or cause an object ball or the cue ball to contact a cushion. Failure to meet these requirements is a foul. Any legally pocketed ball entitles shooter to continue at the table until he fails to pocket an object ball on a shot (see exception: rule of play number 4).

3. If the player pockets any opponent's balls on an illegal shot, they are spotted; but if he pockets his own group balls on an illegal shot, they remain pocketed. If player pockets the last ball of his own group, whether or not on a legal shot, it remains pocketed and his inning ends.

4. When a player's last group ball is legally pocketed, he is eliminated from the shooting rotation. He remains eliminated for the duration of the game unless a foul is committed by a player still in the game; when a player is reinstated due to a foul, he resumes his normal position in the original order of play.

5. When a player has the cue ball in hand behind the head string (as after a scratch), and all balls of all opponents' groups are behind the head string, the object ball nearest the head string may, at the shooter's request, be spotted on the foot spot. If two or more balls are an equal distance from the head string, the player may designate which of the equidistant balls he desires to be spotted.

6. When successive games are being played, the order of play for the next game is the same as the order of final elimination in the preceding game. (First player eliminated breaks; winner shoots last; others in order of elimination.)

ILLEGALLY POCKETED BALLS. Opponents' group balls are spotted, no penalty. Shooter's group balls remain pocketed, no penalty.

JUMPED OBJECT BALLS. Same as illegally pocketed balls.

CUE BALL AFTER JUMPING OFF THE TABLE OR SCRATCH. Incoming player has cue ball in hand behind the head string.

PENALTY FOR FOULS. Shooter's inning ends. In addition, one ball from each of the opponents' groups that is off the table is brought back into play. Players who had been eliminated can be reinstated at any time until the game is over. If a player's group has no pocketed balls at the time of a foul by one of his opponents, then the penalty has no effect on that group or player; the penalty is not carried forward.

Equal Offense

Except when clearly contradicted by these additional rules, the general rules of pocket billiards apply.

TYPE OF GAME. Equal offense is a game in which each player shoots until he misses a shot, fouls or pockets the maximum amount of balls allowed for the inning. The winner is determined by the total-inning score (similar to bowling). Based on 14.1 continuous, the game is ideal for leagues, tournaments, handicapping and averaging; fair, fun and interesting for beginners as well as the advanced player. Although copyrighted by Jerry Briesath, he has placed no restrictions on its use.

PLAYERS. Any number.

BALLS USED. Standard set of object balls one through fifteen, plus cue ball.

THE RACK. Standard triangle rack; balls placed entirely at random. The balls are racked at the beginning of each inning for each player.

OBJECT OF THE GAME. To score more total points than opponent(s) in a predetermined number of innings (200 points in ten innings maximum).

SCORING. Any legally pocketed ball counts one point for shooter.

OPENING BREAK. At the start of each player's inning, he has a free break (no special balls to cushion or other requirements once break stroke commences, and a jumped or scratched cue ball is without penalty). Any balls pocketed on the break are spotted, and player then begins shooting with object balls in position and cue ball in hand behind the head string. The opening break takes place at the start of every inning of each player (ten times per match in championship play for each player).

RULES OF PLAY.

1. Player may shoot any ball he chooses, but before he shoots must designate an object ball and a called pocket. He need not indicate kisses, caroms, combinations or cushions (none of which are illegal). A legally pocketed ball entitles the shooter to continue at the table until he fails to pocket a called ball, or until he has scored the maximum total per inning permissible (twenty points in championship play).

2. Player is entitled to any additional balls pocketed on a shot, as long as he pockets his called ball.

3. Shooting order for subsequent innings is determined by the scoring results of preceding innings—player with the highest score shooting first. In the event of a tie inning, the order does not change.

4. If players are tied for high match total (ten inning) score, additional innings are played by each tied player with the first player posting a superior score to his opponent(s), in an equal number of innings, being the winner (sudden death).

JUMPED OBJECT BALLS. All spotted; no penalty. Player remains at the table if he has legally pocketed a called ball.

CUE BALL AFTER JUMPING OFF THE TABLE OR SCRATCH. Does not apply to equal offense, since a jumped or scratched cue ball ends player's inning, and all players' innings begin with the opening break.

PENALTY FOR FOULS. No point penalty; player's inning ends.

SOME VARIATIONS. For purposes of scheduling, handicapping, etc., variations can be made as follows:

1. A given number of misses or fouls may be allowed per inning (use 14.1 continuous rules for cue ball after jump or scratch).

2. Maximum number of balls per inning permissible may be increased or decreased.

3. Number of innings constituting a match may be increased or decreased.

4. Each player's inning may be restricted by a time limit.

5. Combinations of any of the variations above may be utilized, and may be applied in a nonuniform manner as a means of handicapping players.

6. As an exercise for beginners to progress in finding patterns of play, three chances should be allowed (two misses, cue ball in hand) to reach a score of fifteen. An intermediate player should be allowed two chances. The ten-inning perfect score would thus be 150.

7. Third miss ends player's inning.

Fifteen Ball

Except when clearly contradicted by these additional rules, the general rules of pocket billiards apply.

TYPE OF GAME. Fifteen ball is a basic game variation that does not require calling balls or pockets, and yet rewards good shot selection because scoring is based on the numerical values of the balls (numbers) as in rotation. It is a game well suited for developing skills at beginning and intermediate player levels.

PLAYERS. Two or more, though two players are generally preferred.

BALLS USED. Standard set of object balls one through fifteen plus cue ball.

THE RACK. Standard triangle rack with the fifteen ball on the foot spot; other balls have no exact positions, but the higher-numbered balls are placed at the front of the rack near the fifteen ball, with the lower-numbered balls near the back of the rack.

OBJECT OF THE GAME. To score balls of greater total point value than opponent(s).

SCORING. Each legally pocketed object ball has a point value equal to its number. Game ends when a player's point total mathematically eliminates opponent(s) (sixty-one in a two-player game). If two or more players tie for highest point total, the tied player legally pocketing the last object ball is credited with the game.

OPENING BREAK. Starting player must either pocket a ball (does not have to call either ball or pocket), or cause the cue ball to contact an object ball, and then the cue ball and two object balls must contact a cushion. If he fails to do so, incoming player has choice of accepting the table in position and shooting, or having the balls re-racked and shooting the opening break shot himself, or requiring offending player to repeat the opening break.

RULES OF PLAY.

1. Any ball pocketed on a legal shot entitles shooter to continue at the table until he fails to do so.

2. On all shots subsequent to the opening break, player must cause the cue ball to contact an object ball, and then either pocket an object ball, or cause an object ball or the cue ball to contact a cushion. Failure to do so is a foul.

3. When a player has the cue ball in hand behind the head string (as after a scratch) and all object balls are also behind the head string, the object ball nearest the head string may be spotted on the foot spot at his request. If two or more balls are an equal distance from the head string, the player may designate which of the equidistant balls he desires to be spotted.

ILLEGALLY POCKETED BALLS. All spotted; no penalty.

JUMPED OBJECT BALLS. All spotted; no penalty.

CUE BALL AFTER JUMPING OFF THE TABLE OR SCRATCH. Incoming player has cue ball in hand behind the head string.

PENALTY FOR FOULS. Three points are deducted from the offender's score for each foul committed. After fouls other than jumped cue ball or cue-ball scratch, incoming player accepts the table in position.

Forty-One

Except when clearly contradicted by these additional rules, the general rules of pocket billiards apply.

TYPE OF GAME. Forty-one pocket billiards is another game that is well suited for social play at parties or other gatherings where players of mixed abilities will take part. Since no one knows what number "pea" is held by his opponent(s), it is difficult to play defensively. In addition, the rules are designed to greatly equalize all the players' chances. An unusual and interesting game!

PLAYERS. Two to fifteen (though three, four, or five are generally preferred).

BALLS USED. Standard set of object balls one through fifteen plus cue ball. A set of fifteen numbered peas (or pills) and a shake bottle are also used.

THE RACK. Standard triangle rack with balls placed entirely at random.

DETERMINING PRIVATE NUMBERS. After the balls are racked but before play begins, each player is given a pea from the shake bottle containing the peas numbered from one through fifteen. The number of the pea is the player's private number and is kept secret.

OBJECT OF THE GAME. To score points which, when added to the player's private number, total exactly forty-one.

SCORING. Each legally pocketed ball has a point value equal to its number.

OPENING BREAK. Starting player must make an open break. He is not obligated to pocket a ball on the break shot; but if he fails to make a legal open break, it is a foul.

RULES OF PLAY.

1. Any ball(s) scored on a legal stroke count for the shooter. Players may shoot any ball and need not call ball, pocket or mode of shot.

2. A player is permitted only one shot or turn per inning, regardless of whether or not he scores.

3. An illegally pocketed ball is a foul, and does not score for the shooter.

4. On all shots, player must cause the cue ball to contact an object ball and then either pocket an object ball, or cause an object ball or the cue ball to contact a cushion. Failure to do so is a foul.

5. When a player has the cue ball in hand behind the head string (as after a scratch) and all object balls are also behind the head string, the object ball nearest the head string may be spotted on the foot spot at his request. If two or more balls are an equal distance from the head string, the player may designate which of the equidistant balls he desires to be spotted.

6. When player has a total count of forty-one, he must announce his victory and present his pea for confirmation prior to the next player shooting. If he fails to declare his forty-one total until the next player has shot, he must wait until his next turn to so declare. If, in the meantime, another player succeeds in attaining a legal total count of forty-one and properly declares, the latter player wins the game.

7. If a player totals more than forty-one points, he has "burst" and must so declare immediately (before next shooter plays). All balls the burst player had pocketed are spotted, and the burst player may request a new pea prior to his next turn if he so desires. Any player who bursts and does not declare it prior to the following player's shot is disqualified from further play in the game; if a two-player game, his opponent is automatically the winner.

8. If all balls are pocketed prior to any player attaining a total count of forty-one, the player whose count is closest to forty-one wins

OTHER GAMES

93

the game. If two or more players are tied for nearest to forty-one in this situation, the game is a tie.

ILLEGALLY POCKETED BALLS. All spotted; no penalty.

JUMPED OBJECT BALLS. All spotted; no penalty.

CUE BALL AFTER JUMPING OFF THE TABLE OR SCRATCH. Incoming player has cue ball in hand behind the head string.

PENALTY FOR FOULS. The player committing a foul must spot one of his previously scored object balls for each foul committed. If a player has no previously pocketed balls to his credit when he commits a foul, he is exempt from a penalty for that particular foul.

Honolulu

Except when clearly contradicted by these additional rules, the general rules of pocket billiards apply.

TYPE OF GAME. Honolulu is a unique and fascinating pocket-billiard game that confronts the player with an unending kaleidoscope of strategic and shot-making challenges.

Essentially, Honolulu is just a game of one-rack call shot. Call any ball in any pocket; score one point per legally pocketed ball; the first player to make eight points wins. Said score, incidentally, being kept the same as in one pocket: Put your balls in your bin (just pick a side) and re-spot out of your bin any time you scratch or foul.

The major critical difference being—absolutely no "straight-in" shots are allowed. Each and every legally pocketed ball must be made by means of either a bank, a combination, a carom, a "kick" shot, or some combination thereof.

PLAYERS. Two, or two teams.

BALLS USED. Standard set of fifteen object balls, plus cue ball.

THE RACK. Standard triangle; balls racked at random.

OBJECT OF GAME. Winner of game must score eight points before opponent. (Each legally pocketed ball scores one point.)

SCORING. Player must call ball and pocket. If called ball is made in designated pocket by means of either a bank, combination, carom, or kick shot (or any combination thereof), it is considered a legally pocketed ball and scores one point. It is not necessary to call or specify kisses, caroms, rails, etc. Only called balls legally score. Any balls accidentally (or illegally) pocketed are re-spotted at end of inning. Note: 1985 Vaso Amendment may be implemented at a player's option. Shooter may call any number of balls (two or more) on any one shot, but all balls called must be pocketed, or none are scored. In other words, call all you want, but make all you call—or none

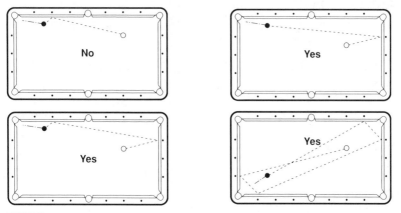

FIGURE 9-4

qualify. A shooter calling two balls but pocketing only one loses inning and must re-spot pocketed ball.

KICK SHOTS. No short-rail kicks. Kick shots are legal only when the cue ball is first banked off of a rail not connected with the designated pocket, or if the cue ball is banked off any two or more rails before striking object ball (see fig. 9-4).

OPENING BREAK. On the opening break the shooter must either call and pocket a call out of the rack, or cause two object balls plus the cue ball to hit the cushion after striking rack with cue ball. Failure to do either is a foul. Penalty: One point. Incoming player accepts cue ball where it lies. Breaker owes one ball (i.e., he must re-spot first ball he legally pockets).

All subsequent play is subject to standard BCA Pocket-Billiard Regulations. (Legal safety: Contact between cue ball and object ball, after which either cue ball, object ball, or both hit a cushion.)

FOULS AND PENALTIES. One point penalty (one ball either re-spotted or owed) per scratch or foul. Following scratch, incoming player has cue ball in hand in kitchen; following foul, incoming shooter accepts cue ball where it lies.

The accidental touching or moving of any ball on the table is considered a foul.

In Honolulu there is no three-consecutive-foul penalty.

ILLEGALLY POCKETED BALLS. Are all re-spotted at end of inning.

Line-Up

Except when clearly contradicted by these additional rules, the general rules of pocket billiards apply.

TYPE OF GAME. Line-up is a forerunner of 14.1 continuous. This is how they did it way back then!

PLAYERS. Two.

BALLS USED. Standard set of object balls numbered one through fifteen, plus cue ball.

THE RACK. Standard triangle rack with the front apex ball on the foot spot, one ball on the rack's right corner, five ball on left corner; other balls placed at random.

OBJECT OF THE GAME. To score the predetermined point total (usually 150 in tournaments, or any agreed upon total) for game prior to opponent.

SCORING. Any ball legally pocketed counts one point for shooter.

OPENING BREAK. Starting player must pocket a called ball or drive two object balls to a cushion. If he fails to do so, he is assessed a two point penalty. Incoming player may accept the table in position and shoot, or require that offender repeat the opening break until the requirements are satisfied. Each successive failure is a two point penalty for offending player.

RULES OF PLAY.

1. A legally pocketed ball entitles shooter to continue at the table until he fails to pocket a called ball on a shot. Player may shoot any ball he chooses, but before he shoots, must designate the ball he will pocket and the pocket into which the ball will score; he need indicate no other detail.

2. On all shots, player must cause the cue ball to contact an object ball and then either pocket an object ball or cause the cue ball or any object ball to contact a cushion. Failure to do so is a foul.

3. A player may call a safety rather than an object ball if he so desires (for defensive purposes). Safety play is legal, but must comply with all applicable rules. Player's inning ends when safety is played, and pocketed balls are not scored. Any object ball pocketed on a called safety is spotted.

4. When the fifteenth ball of the rack has been pocketed, shooter records his scored balls from the rack. The balls are then spotted, and player continues shooting, playing the cue ball from where it came to rest after preceding shot, before the balls were spotted. If player misses or fouls during the rack, he records his score and incoming player shoots, accepting the table in position.

ILLEGALLY POCKETED BALLS. All spotted; no penalty.

JUMPED OBJECT BALLS. All spotted; no penalty.

CUE BALL AFTER JUMPING OFF THE TABLE OR SCRATCH. Incoming player has cue ball in hand behind the head string (unless the foul was a third successive foul; see successive fouls penalty below).

PENALTY FOR FOULS. One point is deducted from offender's score for each foul committed, unless the foul is a third successive foul (see successive fouls penalty below). After fouls other than cue-ball jump, cue-ball scratch, or third successive foul, incoming player accepts the table in position.

SUCCESSIVE FOULS PENALTY. If a player commits three successive fouls, he is penalized one point for each foul, and an additional deduction of fifteen points. The balls are re-racked and offending player is required to break the balls under the requirements of the opening break.

Mr. and Mrs.

Except when clearly contradicted by these additional rules, the general rules of pocket billiards apply.

TYPE OF GAME. Mr. and Mrs. (also called boy meets girl) is a game that combines the general forms of Rotation and Basic Pocket Billiards. The rules are different for players of widely differing skill levels.

PLAYERS. Any number from two to six.

BALLS USED. Standard set of object balls numbered one through fifteen, plus cue ball.

THE RACK. Standard triangle rack with the one ball on the foot spot, two ball on racker's right corner, three ball on left corner, fifteen ball in the center. All other balls are placed at random.

OBJECT OF THE GAME. To score balls of greater total point value than opponent(s).

SCORING. Each legally pocketed object ball has a point value equal to its number. Game ends when a player's point total mathematically eliminates opponents(s)—sixty-one points in a two-player game. If two or more players tie for highest point total, the tied player who legally pocketed the last object ball is credited with a game won.

OPENING BREAK. Starting player must cause the cue ball's first contact to be with the one ball. If starting player fails to meet this requirement, incoming player has the choice of accepting the table in position and shooting or requiring that the balls be re-racked and the offending player repeat the opening break.

RULES OF PLAY.

1. A legally pocketed ball entitles shooter to continue at the table until he fails to legally pocket a ball.

2. On all shots, the more skilled player must cause the cue ball's first contact to be with the lowest-numbered object ball on the table and then either pocket a ball or cause the cue ball or any object ball to contact a cushion. Failure to do so is a foul.

3. The less skilled player may shoot any ball he chooses, regardless of number. He need not call ball, pocket or mode of shot. Any ball pocketed on a legal shot is a scored ball.

4. Player loses game if he commits three successive fouls. If more than a two-player game, balls previously pocketed by disqualified player(s) remain off the table.

5. When a skilled player has the cue ball in hand behind the head string (as after a scratch) and the legal object ball is also behind the head string, the object ball may be spotted on the foot spot at his request.

6. When a less skilled player has the cue ball in hand behind the head string (as after a scratch) and all of the object balls are also behind the head string, the object ball nearest the head string may be spotted at his request. If two or more object balls are an equal distance from the head string, he may also designate which of the equidistant object balls he desires to be spotted.

ILLEGALLY POCKETED BALLS. All spotted; no penalty.

JUMPED OBJECT BALLS. All spotted; no penalty.

CUE BALL AFTER JUMPING OFF THE TABLE OF SCRATCH. Incoming player has cue ball in hand behind the head string.

PENALTY FOR FOULS. No point penalty. If foul is other than jumped cue ball or cue ball scratch, incoming player accepts the cue ball in position. A third consecutive foul by the same player is loss of game.

Pea (Kelly) Pool

Except when clearly contradicted by these additional rules, the general rules of pocket billiards apply.

TYPE OF GAME. Pea (or Kelly) pool is an old favorite among pocket-billiard players who enjoy a group game in which the competitors play individually, and which entails a bit of luck (not so much in the actual play but rather in the "pea" or "pill" each player receives during each game). The game is very popular since it can accommodate players of widely differing levels of ability.

PLAYERS. Two or more, with the best game being from four to six.

BALLS USED. Standard set of object balls numbered one through fifteen, plus cue ball. A set of fifteen numbered peas (or pills) and a shake bottle are also used.

THE RACK. Standard triangle rack with the 1 ball on the foot spot, two ball on racker's right corner, three ball on left corner; all other balls placed at random.

DETERMINING PRIVATE NUMBERS. After the balls are racked, but before play begins, each player is given a pea from the shake bottle (containing the peas numbered one through fifteen). The number of the pea is the player's private number and is kept secret.

OBJECT OF THE GAME. To legally pocket the object ball with the numerical value equivalent to the player's private number.

SCORING. No point value for object balls except the ball equivalent to the pocketing player's private number; when a player legally pockets that object ball, he wins the game. (Option: Game is played until a player legally pockets "his own" ball and wins; as above, he receives two points from each player for winning the game. In addition, when any player's private-number ball is legally pocketed by any player other than himself, the pocketing player receives one point and the player whose ball was pocketed loses one point. Players whose private-number balls have been pocketed by other players continue to shoot in the regular rotation, but if a player fails to announce that his object ball was pocketed by another player prior to a subsequent shot being taken, the offending player is disqualified from further play during the game, and the forfeiture of points to the pocketing player is increased from one to two. If no player succeeds in pocketing his private-number ball, the game ends when the last private-number ball is pocketed, and another game is played with all point values doubled and player who pocketed the last private-number ball being the starting player.)

OPENING BREAK. Starting player must make an open break. If he fails to do so, incoming player has choice of either cue ball in hand behind the head string and table in position, or having the balls re-racked and shooting the opening break shot himself.

RULES OF PLAY.

1. A legally pocketed ball entitles shooter to continue at the table until he fails to legally pocket a ball.

2. On all shots, the cue ball's first contact must be with the lowest-numbered object ball on the table and then must either pocket a ball, or cause the cue ball or any object ball to contact a cushion. Failure to do so is a foul.

3. A player legally pocketing a ball must shoot again. He may not call a safety and spot a pocketed ball.

4. When a player has the cue ball in hand behind the head string (as after a scratch) and the legal object ball is also behind the head string, the object ball may be spotted on the foot spot at his request.

ILLEGALLY POCKETED BALLS. All spotted; no penalty.

JUMPED OBJECT BALLS. All spotted; no penalty.

CUE BALL AFTER JUMPING OFF THE TABLE OR SCRATCH. Incoming player has cue ball in hand behind the head string.

PENALTY FOR FOULS. No point penalty. Incoming player has choice of either accepting the table in position and shooting, or requiring offending player to shoot again (if cue ball is in hand behind the head string, it is so for either player).

Six Ball

Except when clearly contradicted by these additional rules, the general rules of pocket billiards apply.

TYPE OF GAME. Six ball is a variation of rotation in which the lowest-numbered ball on the table must always be the player's first cue-ball contact. If a player complies, any pocketed ball counts. For example, if a player strikes the one ball legally, which then caroms into the six ball and causes it to be pocketed, that player wins the game. It's fast, and with only six object balls on the table, single inning racks are very common!

PLAYERS. Two or more, though two players are generally preferred.

BALLS USED. Object balls one through six, plus cue ball.

THE RACK. Triangle rack (rows of 1-2-3) with the one ball on the foot spot, and the 6 ball in the center of the rear row. All other balls placed entirely at random.

OBJECT OF THE GAME. To legally pocket the six ball.

SCORING. The balls have no point value. The player legally pocketing the six ball is credited with a game won.

OPENING BREAK. The starting player must make an open break or legally pocket an object ball. If he fails to do so, the incoming player has the choice of cue ball in hand behind the head string and object balls in position or having the balls re-racked and shooting the opening break shot himself.

RULES OF PLAY.

1. A legal shot requires that the cue ball's first contact be with the lowest-numbered ball on the table. A player must then pocket a ball or cause the cue ball or any object ball to contact a cushion. Failure to do so is a foul.

2. A legally pocketed ball entitles a shooter to remain at the table until he fails to pocket a ball on a legal shot.

3. When a player legally pockets a ball, he must shoot again. He may not call a safety and spot a legally pocketed object ball.

4. It is a loss of game if a player commits three successive fouls.

ILLEGALLY POCKETED BALLS. All spotted; no penalty. (Common option, coin-operated play: none spotted except game ball.)

JUMPED OBJECT BALLS. All spotted; no penalty.

CUE BALL AFTER JUMPING OFF THE TABLE OR SCRATCH. Incoming player has cue ball in hand behind the head string.

PENALTY FOR FOULS. Incoming player is awarded cue ball in hand behind the head string. However, if it is a third consecutive foul, the rule of 8.4 provides for a penalty of loss of game.

SNOOKER GAMES

Pocket-billiard games in America in the 1800s generally evolved from English billiards (with two cue balls and one red ball) which was played on a 6-by-12-foot table with rails that sloped into the pocket openings. By 1860, New York table manufacturer, author and noted player Michael Phelan replaced the sloping sides of the pockets with straight corners, thus changing the direction of American pocket billiards from the English game from that time to the present.

English billiards could only be played with two players, so eventually multi-player variations such as life pool and pyramid pool became popular in America, England, and territories in which English soldiers were stationed. Life pool featured different-colored balls used as both cue balls and/or object balls depending on the situation and the number of players. Pyramid pool featured fifteen red balls racked on the pyramid (foot) spot, and each player received one point for each red he legally potted. Black pool was a form of pyramid pool which used the black ball from a life pool set so that a player could alternately pot a red and then attempt the black for extra points. Legend has it that in 1875, Sir Neville Chamberlain, an English regiment soldier stationed in Jubbulpore, India, was playing black pool with his fellow officers when he got an idea to add other colored balls to the game so that the variation eventually featured fifteen red balls, a yellow, green, pink and black ball [a blue and brown ball were added some years later]. In the course of play one day a visiting military cadet remarked that first-year cadets at his particular academy were known as "snookers." When the cadet missed a particularly easy pot, Chamberlain exclaimed to him, "Why, you're a regular snooker!" After explaining the meaning of the word to his fellow peers, officer Chamberlain added that perhaps they were all snookers at the game. The term was adopted for this particular variation, and the game has been called snooker ever since.

Snooker spread to other posts, and soldiers returning to England introduced the game there. Champion player John Roberts, Jr. learned the rules of the game on one of his exhibition tours of India, and he may have had some influence in further popularizing the game in the United Kingdom. When English billiards started losing spectator interest at professional matches in England in the 1930s, champion billiardist Joe Davis recognized snooker as a more appealing alternative, and his cue prowess at the game eventually led to snooker being embraced as the more popular championship discipline in that country.

Snooker has never gained as much popularity in the United States, but its appeal to many American players, its rank as the number-one televised sport on English television, and the skillful variations it has bred around the world warrant the inclusion of three pertinent sets of rules in this section.

International Snooker

TYPE OF GAME. International or English snooker is the most widely played form of snooker around the world. It is generally played on 6 by 12 ft. English billiard tables, with cushions that are more narrow than on pocket-billiard tables and which curve smoothly into the pocket openings. 5 by 10 and snooker tables of even smaller playing dimensions may be used for the game. On a 6 by 12 snooker (English billiard table) table the playing area within the cushion faces shall measure 11' 8½" by 5' 10" with a tolerance on both dimensions of ±½".

PLAYERS. Two.

BALLS USED. Set of snooker balls: fifteen object balls that are not numbered and are solid red (called reds), six object balls that may or may not be numbered (called colors), and a cue ball. Point values for object balls: yellow-two, green-three, brown-four, blue-five, pink-six, black-seven. In International Snooker the balls used are 2¹⁄₁₆" diameter.

THE RACK. Play begins with balls placed as in figure 10–1. The pink is spotted on the pyramid spot. The apex ball of the triangle of reds is racked as close as possible to the pink without touching it.

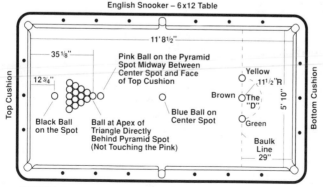

FIGURE 10–1

BALKLINE AND BALK. A straight line drawn twenty-nine inches from the face of the bottom cushion and parallel to it is called the balkline and the intervening spaced is termed the balk.

THE "D." The "D" is a semicircle described in balk with its center at the middle of the balkline and with a radius of 11½ inches. When the striker has cue ball in hand within the D he may place the base of the cue ball anywhere on the line or within the D, and may use his hand or any part of his cue (including the tip) to position the cue ball, as long as it is judged that he is not attempting to play a stroke.

OBJECT OF THE GAME. To score a greater number of points than opponent.

SCORING. Points are scored in two ways: players are awarded points for fouls by the opponent (see penalties for fouls below), and by legally potting reds and/or colors. Each legally potted red ball has a point value of one; each legally potted color ball has a point value as indicated (balls used, above). A frame ends when all balls have been potted, following the rules of play; if, however, only the black (seven) ball is left on the table, the frame ends with the first score or foul. If the players' scores are equal after that scoring, the black ball is spotted on its original position and the players lag or draw lots for the choice of playing at, or assigning opponent to play at, the black ball with the cue ball in hand within the D; the first score or foul then ends the frame.

OPENING BREAK. Players lag or draw lots for choice of break in the opening frame. In a match format the players alternate the break in subsequent frames. Starting player has cue ball in hand within the D. He must cause the cue ball to contact a red ball. It is not necessary to send a ball to a rail or into a pocket. Failure to meet this requirement is a foul (see penalties for fouls). A foul is scored and, as with all fouls, the incoming player has the choice of accepting the table and becoming the striker, or requiring offender to break again.

RULES OF PLAY.

1. A legally potted ball entitles the striker to continue at the table until he fails to legally pot a ball.

2. On all shots, the striker must comply with the appropriate requirements of Rules #5 & #6. It is not necessary to cause the cue ball or an object ball to contact a cushion or drop in a pocket after the cue ball has contacted a legal object ball (ball on). Failure to contact a legal object ball first is a foul.

3. As long as reds are on the table, the incoming striker (player taking his first stroke of an inning) always has a red as his legal object ball (ball on).

4. Any red balls potted on a legal shot are legally potted balls; the striker need not call any particular red ball(s), pocket(s) or details of how the pot will be played.

5. When the striker has a red ball as his ball on (legal object ball), he must cause the cue ball's first contact to be with a red ball. Failure to do so is a foul (see penalties for fouls).

6. After the striker has scored a red ball initially, his next legal object is a colored ball, and as long as reds remain on the table he must alternate his play between reds and colors (though within each group he may play ball of his choice). When reds remain on the table and a color is his object, the striker must designate prior to stroking which color ball is his object (that specific color is then his ball on), and cause the cue ball's first contact with a ball to be with that colored ball. If the striker fails to meet these requirements, it is a foul (see penalties for fouls).

7. If the striker's ball on is a red, and he pots a color, it is a foul.

8. If the striker's ball on is a color, and he pots any other ball, it is a foul.

9. Jump shots are illegal in international snooker. It is a foul if the striker intentionally causes the cue ball to jump (rise from the bed of the table) by any means, if the jump is an effort to clear an obstructing ball.

10. While reds remain on the table, each potted color ball is spotted prior to the next stroke (see spotting balls, below, for spotting rules). After a color has been spotted, if the striker plays while that ball is incorrectly spotted (and opponent or referee calls it before two such plays have been taken), the shot taken is a foul. If the striker plays two strokes after such an error without it being announced by the opponent or referee, he is free of penalty and continues playing and scoring normally as though the spotting error simply had not occurred. The striker is responsible for ensuring that all balls are correctly spotted before striking. If the striker plays while a ball(s) is not on the table that should be, a fouls may be awarded whenever the foul is discovered during the striker's inning. Any scoring prior to the discovery of the foul will count.

11. When no reds remain on the table, the striker's balls on become the colors, in ascending numerical order (2,3,4,5,6,7). These legally potted colors are not spotted after each is potted; they remain off the table (the black (seven) ball is an exception in the case of a tie score: see scoring).

ILLEGALLY POTTED BALL. Reds illegally potted are not spotted; they remain off the table. Colors illegally potted are spotted (see spotting balls, below).

OBJECT BALLS JUMPED OFF THE TABLE. Reds jumped off the table are not spotted and the striker has committed a foul. Colors jumped off the table are spotted and the striker has committed a foul (see penalties for fouls, below).

SPOTTING BALLS. Reds are never spotted. Colors to be spotted are placed as at the start of the game. If a color's spot is occupied (to mean that to spot it would make it touch a ball), it is placed on the spot of the highest value color that is unoccupied. If all spots are occupied, the color is spotted as close as possible to its original spot on a straight line between its spot and the nearest point on the top (foot) cushion.

CUE BALL AFTER JUMPING OFF THE TABLE OR SCRATCH. Incoming player has cue ball in hand within the D. When cue ball is in hand within the D (except on the opening break), there is no restriction (based on position of reds or colors) as to what balls may be played; striker may play at any ball on regardless of where it is on the table.

TOUCHING A BALL. While balls are in play it is a foul if the striker touches any object ball or if the striker touches the cue ball with anything other than the cue tip during a legal stroke.

SNOOKERED. The cue ball is snookered when a direct stroke in a straight line to any part of every ball on is obstructed by a ball or balls not on. If there is any one ball that is not so obstructed, the cue ball is not snookered. If in hand within the D, the cue ball is snookered only if obstructed from all positions on or within the D. If the cue ball is obstructed by more than one ball, the one nearest to the cue ball is the effective snookering ball.

ANGLED. The cue ball is angled when a direct stroke in a straight line to any part of every ball on is obstructed by a corner of the cushion. If there is any one ball on that is not so obstructed, the cue ball is not angled. If angled after a foul the referee or player will state "angled ball," and the striker has the choice to either play from that position or play from in hand within the D.

OCCUPIED. A spot is said to be occupied if a ball cannot be placed on it without it touching another ball.

TOUCHING BALL. If the cue ball is touching another ball which is, or can be, on, the referee or player shall state "touching ball." Thereafter the striker must play away from it or it is a push stroke (foul). No penalty is incurred for thus playing away if the ball is not on; the ball is on and the striker nominates such ball; or the ball is on and the striker nominates, and first hits, another ball. (If the referee considers that a touching ball has moved through an agency other than the player, it is not a foul.)

PUSH STROKE. A push stroke is a foul and is made when the tip of the cue remains in contact with the cue ball when the cue ball makes contact with the object ball, or after the cue ball has commenced its forward motion. Provided that where the cue ball and an object ball are almost touching, it shall be deemed a legal stroke if the cue ball hits the finest possible edge of the object ball.

MISS. The striker shall to the best of his ability endeavor to hit the ball on. If the referee considers the rule infringed he shall call foul and "miss." The incoming player may play the ball(s) as it lies, or may request that the ball(s) be returned to the original position and have the offending player play the stroke again. Note: if the ball on cannot possibly be hit, the striker is judged to be attempting to hit the ball on.

FREE BALL. After a foul, if the cue ball is snookered, the referee or player shall state "free ball." If the nonoffending player takes the next stroke he may nominate any ball as on. For this stroke, such ball shall be regarded as, and acquire the value of, the ball on. It is a foul should the cue ball fail to first hit, or, when only pink and black remain on the table, be snookered by, the free ball. If the free ball is potted, it is spotted, and the value of the ball on is scored. If the ball on is potted it is scored. If both the free ball and the ball on are potted, only the value of the ball on is scored.

FOULS. If a foul is committed:
1. The player who committed the foul incurs the penalty prescribed (which is added to the opponent's score), and has to play again if requested by the next player. Once such a request has been made it cannot be withdrawn.
2. Should more than one foul be committed in the same stroke, the highest-value penalty shall be incurred.
3. Any ball improperly spotted shall remain where positioned, except that if off the table it shall be correctly spotted.

PENALTIES FOR FOULS. The following are fouls and incur a penalty of four points or the higher one prescribed.
(1) Value of the ball on—
   By striking
   a. When the balls are still moving from the previous shot.
   b. The cue ball more than once (double hit).
   c. Without at least one foot on the floor.
   d. Out of turn.
   e. Improperly from in hand within the D.
   By causing
   f. The cue ball to miss all object balls.
   g. The cue ball to enter a pocket.
   h. A snooker with free ball.
   i. A jump shot.

(2) Value of the ball on or ball concerned—
By causing
   a. A ball not on to enter a pocket.
   b. The cue ball to first hit a ball not on.
   c. A push stroke.
   d. By striking with a ball not correctly spotted.
   e. By touching a ball with other than the tip of the cue.
   f. By forcing a ball off the table.

(3) Value of the ball on or higher value of the two balls by causing the cue ball to hit simultaneously two balls other than two reds or a free ball and the ball on.

(4) Penalty of seven points is incurred if—
The striker
   a. After potting a red commits a foul before nominating a color.
   b. Uses a ball off the table for any purpose.
   c. Plays at reds in successive strokes.
   d. Uses as the cue ball any ball other than the white one.

American Snooker

TYPE OF GAME. American snooker is a "cousin" of snooker as it is played widely around the world, the rules giving it a distinct orientation toward the structure of many American pocket-billiard games. It is generally played on either 5 by 10 or 6 by 12 snooker tables, with cushions that are narrower than other pocket-billiard tables, and curve smoothly into the pocket openings. The balls used are either 2$\frac{1}{16}$" or 2$\frac{1}{8}$" diameter. (See BCA specifications.)

PLAYERS. Two.

BALLS USED. Set of snooker balls: Fifteen object balls that are not numbered and are solid red (called reds), six object balls that may or may not be numbered (called colors) and a cue ball. Point values for object balls: yellow-two, green-three, brown-four, blue-five, pink-six, black-seven.

THE RACK. Play begins with balls placed as in figure 10–2.

OBJECT OF THE GAME. To score a greater number of points than opponent.

SCORING. Points are scored in two ways: players are awarded points for fouls by the opponent (see penalty for foul, below), and by legally pocketing reds and/or colors. Each legally pocketed red ball has a point value of one; each legally pocketed color ball has a point value as indicated (balls used, above). Game ends when all balls have been pocketed, following the rules of play; if, however, only the black (seven) ball is left on the table, the game ends with the first score or

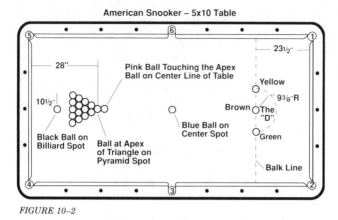

Pink Ball Touching the Apex
Ball on Center Line of Table

28"

Yellow

101/2"

93/8"R

Brown

The
"D"

Black Ball on
Billiard Spot

Blue Ball on
Center Spot

Green

Ball at Apex
of Triangle on
Pyramid Spot

Balk Line

231/2"

FIGURE 10–2

SNOOKER GAMES

(109)

foul. If the players' scores are equal after that scoring, the black ball is spotted on its original position and the players lag for the choice of shooting at, or assigning opponent to shoot at the black ball with the cue ball in hand within the D; the first score or foul then ends the game.

OPENING BREAK. Starting player has cue ball in hand within the D. He must cause the cue ball to contact a red ball prior to contacting a color, cause a red ball to contact a cushion or drop into a pocket, and cause the cue ball to contact a cushion after it contacts a red ball. Failure to meet these requirements is a foul and a breaking violation. A foul is scored and incoming player has choice of accepting the table and shooting, or requiring offender to break again.

RULES OF PLAY.

1. A legally pocketed ball entitles shooter to continue at the table until he fails to legally pocket a ball.

2. On all shots, player must comply with the appropriate requirements of Rules #5 & #6, plus cause the cue ball or an object ball to contact a cushion or drop in a pocket after the cue ball has contacted a legal object ball (on ball). Failure to do so is a foul.

3. As long as reds are on the table, an incoming player (player taking his first shot of an inning) always has a red as his legal object ball (on ball).

4. Any red balls pocketed on a legal shot are legally pocketed balls; player need not call any particular red ball(s), pocket(s) or mode of pocketing.

5. When a player has a red ball as his on ball (required legal object ball), he must cause the cue ball's first contact to be with a red ball. Failure to do so is a foul. Rule #2 also applies.

6. After a player has scored a red ball, his next legal object is a color, and as long as reds remain on the table he must alternate his play between reds and colors (though within each group he may play ball of his choice). When reds remain on the table and a color is his object, the player must designate prior to shooting which color ball is his object (that specific color is then his on ball), and cause the cue ball's first contact with a ball to be with that color ball. If player fails to meet these requirements, it is a foul. Rule #2 requirements also apply.

7. If player's on ball is a red, and he pockets a color, it is a foul.

8. If player's on ball is a color, and he pockets any other ball, it is a foul.

9. It is a foul if a player intentionally causes the cue ball to jump (rise from the bed of the table) by any means, if the jump is an effort to clear an obstructing ball.

10. While reds remain on the table, each pocketed color ball is spotted prior to the next stroke. (See spotting balls, below, for spotting rules). If player shooting after a color has been spotted plays while that ball is incorrectly spotted (and opponent or referee calls it before two such shots have been taken), the shot taken is a foul. If such shooting player shoots twice after such error without it being announced by opponent or referee, he is free of penalty and continues shooting and scoring normally as though the spotting error simply had not occurred.

11. When no reds remain on the table, player's on balls become the colors, in ascending numerical order (2,3,4,5,6,7). These legally pocketed colors are not spotted after each is pocketed; they remain off the table (the seven ball is an exception in the case of a tie score: see scoring).

ILLEGALLY POCKETED BALLS. Reds illegally pocketed are not spotted; they remain off the table. Colors illegally pocketed are spotted (see spotting balls).

JUMPED OBJECT BALLS. Reds jumped off the table are not spotted; no penalty. Colors jumped off the table are spotted; no penalty.

SPOTTING BALLS. Reds are never spotted. Colors to be spotted are placed as at the start of the game. If a color's spot is occupied (to mean that to spot it would make it touch another ball), it is placed on the spot of the highest value color that is unoccupied. If all spots are occupied, the color is spotted as close as possible to its original spot on a straight line between its spot and the nearest point on the foot cushion.

CUE BALL AFTER JUMPING OFF THE TABLE OR SCRATCH.
Incoming player has cue ball in hand within the D. When cue ball is

in hand within the D (except on the opening break), there is no restriction (based on position of reds or colors) as to what balls may be played; player may play any on ball regardless of where it is on the table.

PENALTY FOR FOULS. Seven points are added to nonfouling player's score for each foul committed (no deduction from offender's score). Incoming (nonoffending) player has the choice of either accepting the table in position and shooting, or requiring the offending player to shoot again; if the foul is a cue ball jumped off the table or a cue ball scratch, the cue ball is in hand within the D for either player. If the foul is other than cue ball jumped off the table or scratch, the cue ball remains in position.

Golf

TYPE OF GAME. In many sections of the United States the most popular game on a snooker table is golf. It is usually played on a 5 by 10 or 6 by 12 snooker table with either 2⅛″ or 2¹⁄₁₆″ diameter snooker balls (see BCA specifications).

PLAYERS. Two or more, with a game often including four players or more.

BALLS USED. The numbered group of snooker balls (two-yellow through seven-black) and a white snooker cue ball.

THE RACK. Starting player's object ball is spotted on the foot (pyramid) spot.

OBJECT OF THE GAME. For a player to successfully pocket his object ball in each of the six pockets in numerical pocket order (see fig. 10–2) before his opponent(s) does.

DETERMINING ORDER OF PLAY. Players draw lots (or numbered peas) from a shake bottle. Lowest-drawn number goes first with the remainder of the order corresponding to the ascending draw of peas for each player. Starting player's object ball throughout the game is the two ball (yellow); the next player, the three ball (green); the next player, the four ball (brown); etc.

SCORING. The balls have no numerical value for scoring. The first player to follow the rules of play and legally pocket his object ball in the six (side) pocket wins the game. Players keep track of the number of fouls (known as hickeys) each competitor accrues throughout the game. A hickey may be assigned any value, and players must determine the differences in the totals of hickeys due at the end of each game. For example, if the winning Player A has six hickeys, Player B has four hickeys, and Player C has ten hickeys, Player A's hickeys are irrelevant. Player B owes Player A the value of four hickeys and Player C owes Player A the value of ten hickeys.

Usually the game itself has a value and Player A receives that value from each player for winning the game.

OPENING BREAK. Starting player begins play with the cue ball on or within the D and his object ball (for the starting player, the yellow two ball) on the foot spot. His objective is to pocket his ball in pocket one. If the first player misses, the second player takes the cue ball in hand within the D, positions his object ball (three-the green) on the foot spot and attempts to pocket it in pocket one. If the second players misses, the third player takes cue ball in hand within the D, positions his object ball (four-the brown) on the foot spot, and attempts to pocket it in pocket one. Subsequent players follow the same procedure to enter the game. If a player pockets his first shot into pocket one, his object ball is respotted on the foot spot and the player shoots again to pocket his object ball in pocket two from wherever the cue ball comes to rest. Once his inning is complete, the next player entering the game takes cue ball in hand within the D and starts play as described above.

SUBSEQUENT HOLES. After all players have entered the game (unless a player runs out the game from his break) the cue ball is played from wherever it comes to rest after each player's shot for the remainder of the game (see below if jumped or scratched). Once a player pockets his object ball in pocket one, the object ball is respotted on the foot spot, and the player continues shooting for pocket two. When he misses, the next player shoots at his object ball. A player must successfully complete all six holes, playing in order, in this manner. The player who completes this pattern first wins the game.

RULES OF PLAY.

1. It is a foul to pocket the object ball in any pocket other than the one in which the player is attempting to score.

2. On all shots it is necessary for the player to hit his object ball first.

3. For a legal shot, a player is required to either send the cue ball to a rail and then hit his object ball first, hit his object ball first and pocket it, or hit his object ball first and send any ball to a cushion.

4. It is a foul to strike, touch or in any way make contact with the cue ball in play or any object balls in play with anything (the body, clothing, chalk, mechanical bridge, cue shaft, etc.) except the cue tip (while attached to the cue shaft), which may contact the cue ball in the execution of a legal shot.

5. It is a foul to hit another player's object ball first. If a player hits an opponent's object ball first, the player loses his turn, is credited with a hickey, and the opponent has the choice of returning the object ball to its original position.

6. If a player has a clear shot at his full object ball and misses the entire ball, it is a foul (hickey), he loses his turn, and the object ball is spotted on the foot spot.

7. If a player commits a foul and the incoming player is snookered from seeing his entire ball, that player may mark the position(s) of the offending ball(s), remove the obstacle ball(s) from the table, shoot at his object ball, and replace the removed ball(s) to original position(s) immediately after the stroke.

ILLEGALLY POCKETED BALLS. All are spotted on the foot spot, unless an opponent's ball was struck first. Then the opponent may choose to return his object ball to its original position. The stroke is a foul and the offending player receives a hickey.

JUMPED OBJECT BALLS. An object ball that jumps off the table is a foul, and the offending player loses his turn and recieves a hickey. The object ball is spotted on the foot spot unless an opponent's ball was struck first. In that case the opponent may choose to return his object ball to its original position.

CUE BALL AFTER JUMPING OFF THE TABLE OR SCRATCH. The offending player fouls, loses his turn, and receives a hickey. The incoming player has cue ball in hand on or within the D, may shoot in any direction, and may shoot at his object ball if it is in the D as well. Any object balls pocketed on the foul stroke are respotted on the foot spot in numerical order unless an opponent's ball was struck first. In that case the opponent may choose to return his object ball to its original position.

SPOTTING BALLS. After each player has completed his opening break shot, if a player is required to spot a ball on the foot spot, he must do so immediately after the resulting stroke. If the ball cannot be spotted without touching another ball, the ball is spotted as close to it as possible without touching (if the obstacle ball is the cue ball) and frozen to the ball (if the obstacle ball is an object ball), and on the direct line between the foot spot and the foot rail.

GENERAL RULES OF CAROM BILLIARDS

The rules in this section apply generally to all the specific forms and varieties of carom-billiard games included in this rule book. Certain games, however, do have exceptions that supersede and/or modify the general rules; these exceptions are flagged with a parenthetical notation, referencing the particular game or variation in which the general rule might be either modified or nonapplicable. Thus, unless specifically noted otherwise, these general rules apply to all carom-billiard games.

To facilitate the use and understanding of these general rules, many terms that may require definition for some readers are set in italic in their first appearance, so that the reader may refer to the Glossary of Billiard Terms chapter for the exact meaning of the term.

For purposes of simplicity and clarity, masculine pronouns have been utilized throughout this rule book. Obviously, such references should be considered to apply to any player, regardless of gender.

Although most references in these rules are to a player or players, since most carom-billiard games can be adapted to team play, the reader should interpret the rules as equally applicable to a team or teams when appropriate.

The United States Billiard Association today sanctions most United States play of the popular carom game of three-cushion billiards. In the individual game rules for three-cushion, the USBA official rules have been reprinted exactly as published by that group, resulting in some duplication of general rules from this section within the USBA's rules.

TABLES, BALLS, EQUIPMENT. All games are contested on tables, and with balls and equipment meeting the standards prescribed in the BCA specifications.

BALLS DEFINED. Two white balls and a red; each player has a white ball that is a cue ball when he is shooting, while the red is never a cue ball. One of the white balls has two or three small colored spots to differentiate it from the other. (Note: Four ball is played with a fourth ball as well; see four ball rules.)

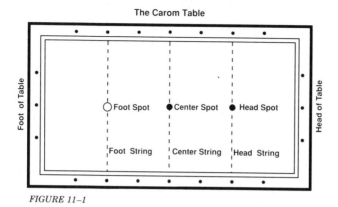

The Carom Table

Foot Spot ● Center Spot ● Head Spot

Foot of Table

Head of Table

Foot String | Center String | Head String

FIGURE 11–1

STRIKING CUE BALL. Legal shots require that the *cue ball* be struck with the *cue tip* only.

DETERMINING FIRST PLAYER. The player to perform the *opening break* shot is determined by either *lag for break* or *lot*. (The lag-for-break procedure is required for formal competition.) The player winning the lag or lot has the choice of performing the opening break shot or assigning it to the opposition.

LAG FOR BREAK. Red ball is spotted on *foot spot* (except in *four ball*). With the *cue balls in hand behind the head string,* one player to the right and one to the left of the *head spot,* the balls are shot to the foot *cushion* and back to the head end of the table. The player whose ball ends up closest to the head cushion wins the lag, subject to the following qualifications:

The lagged ball must contact the foot cushion at least once; other cushion contacts are immaterial except as prohibited below. It is an automatic loss of the lag if the ball crosses into the opponent's half of the table, or the ball fails to contact the foot cushion, or the ball jumps the table, or the ball hits the red ball.

If both players violate automatic-loss lag rules as above, or if the referee is unable to determine which ball is closer, the lag is a tie and is replayed.

The lag for opening break is performed by both players simultaneously, although they need not stroke the lag shots in perfect unison.

CHOICE OF CUE BALLS. The winner of the lag has the choice of cue balls, either the all-white "clear" or the color-marked "spot," which is then used throughout the game. If an odd number of players is competing, the same cue ball is not played throughout the game. Rather, incoming player always plays the cue ball that was not used by the player who immediately precede him (Exception: four-ball caroms).

BALL POSITIONS—OPENING BREAK. The red ball is spotted on

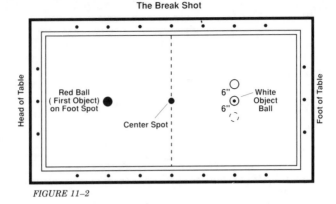

The Break Shot

FIGURE 11–2

the foot spot. Nonbreaking player's cue ball is spotted on the *head spot*. Breaking player's cue ball is placed on the *head string* within six inches (measured to the ball's center) of the head spot. (Note: Four ball uses a different opening-break position.)

RED BALL FIRST OBJECT. Player making opening break shot must contact the red ball first, rather than the opponent's cue ball. If the cue ball on the opening break strikes the other white ball first rather than the red ball, it is an *error* and ends his *inning;* no score is valid. (Exception: four-ball caroms.)

On all subsequent shots, players may make either the red or the white (or "pink" in four ball) ball his first object (first ball struck by the cue ball). (Exception: red ball.)

FOOT ON FLOOR. It is a foul if a player shoots when at least one foot is not in contact with the floor. Foot attire must be normal in regard to size, shape and the manner in which it is worn.

SHOOTING WITH BALLS IN MOTION. It is a foul if a player shoots while the cue ball or any object ball is in motion. A spinning ball is in motion.

COMPLETION OF STROKE. A stroke is not complete and therefore is not counted until all balls on the table have become motionless after the stroke. A spinning ball is in motion.

FOULS BY TOUCHING BALLS. It is a foul to strike, touch or in any way make contact with the cue ball in play or any object balls in play with anything (the body, clothing, chalk, *mechanical bridge, cue shaft,* etc.) except the cue tip (while attached to the cue shaft), which may contact the cue ball once in the execution of a shot.

FOULS BY DOUBLE HITS. It is a foul if the cue ball is struck more than once on a shot by the cue tip. If, in the referee's judgment, the cue ball has left initial contact with the cue tip and then is struck a second time in the course of the same stroke, it is a foul. If the referee judges, by virtue of sound, ball position and action, and stroke used, that there are two separate contacts of the cue ball by the cue tip on a stroke, the stroke is a foul.

PUSH–SHOT FOULS. It is a foul if the cue ball is pushed or shoved by the cue tip, with contact being maintained for more than the momentary time necessary for a stroked shot. If the referee judges that the player put the cue tip against the cue ball and then pushed or shoved on into the shot, maintaining contact beyond the normal momentary split second, the stroke is a foul.

JUMPED CUE BALL. When a stroke results in the cue ball being a *jumped ball,* the stroke is a foul. (Note: Jumped object balls may or may not be fouls; see specific game rules.)

GENERAL RULE, ALL FOULS. Though the penalties for fouls differ from game to game, the following applies to all fouls: player's inning ends, and if on a stroke, the stroke is invalid and cannot be a scoring stroke.

ILLEGAL JUMPING OF BALL. It is a foul if a player strikes the cue ball below center ("digs under" it) and intentionally causes it to rise off the bed of the table (usually in an effort to clear an obstructing ball). Such jumping action may occur accidentally on occasion, and such jumps are not necessarily considered fouls; they may still be ruled foul strokes however, if for example, the ferrule or cue shaft makes contact with the cue ball in the course of the shot.

SPECIAL INTENTIONAL–FOUL PENALTY. The cue ball in play shall not be intentionally struck with anything other than a cue's attached tip (such as the ferrule, shaft, etc.). While such contact is automatically a foul under the provisions of fouls by touching balls, if the referee deems the contact to be intentional, he shall warn the player once during a match that a second violation during that match will result in the loss of the match by forfeiture. If a second violation does occur, the match must be forfeited.

BALLS MOVING SPONTANEOUSLY. If a balls shifts, settles, turns or otherwise moves "by itself," the ball shall remain in the position it assumed and play continues.

PLAYER–RESPONSIBILITY FOULS. The player is responsible for chalk, bridges, files and any other items or equipment he brings to, uses at, or causes to approximate the table. If he drops a pen or a piece of chalk, or knocks off a mechanical bridge head, as examples, he is guilty of a foul should such an object make a contact with a ball in play.

JUMPED BALLS DEFINED. Balls coming to rest other than on the bed of the table after a stroke (on the cushion top, rail surface, floor, etc.) are considered jumped balls. Balls may bounce on the cushion tops, rails or light fixtures of the table in play without being jumped balls if they return to the bed of the table under their own power and without touching anything not a part of the table equipment. The table equipment shall consist of its light fixture and any permanent parts of the table proper. (Balls that strike or touch anything not a part of the table equipment shall be considered jumped balls even though they might return to the bed of the table after contact with the non-equipment item[s]).

All jumped balls are spotted when all balls have stopped moving (see spotting jumped balls, below).

OUTSIDE INTERFERENCE. If the balls are moved (or a player bumped such that play is directly affected) by a nonplayer during a match, the balls shall be replaced as near as possible to their original positions immediately prior to the incident, and play shall resume with no penalty on the player affected. If the match is officiated, the referee shall replace the balls. This rule shall also apply to act-of-God interference, such as earthquake, hurricane, light fixture falling, a power failure, etc.

DEFINITION OF LEGAL SAFETY. Player must drive an object ball to a cushion or cause the cue ball to contact a cushion after striking an object ball. Failure to do so is a foul. (Note: USBA three-cushion rules prohibit all intentional safeties.)

LIMIT ON SAFETY PLAY. Player must not play safety in consecutive innings. When a player's last shot was a safety, he must not play another safety on his next shot. If he does so, it is a foul. (Note: does not apply in USBA three-cushion play.)

PLAYING FROM SAFETY. When a player has either fouled or played an intentional safety on his last shot, he comes to the table for his next shot playing from safety.

Player must make an obvious and legal attempt to score. If he again resorts to safety play, whether or not the effort meets the requirements of a legal safety, he has fouled. (Note: Playing from safety does not apply in three-cushion.)

SPOTTING JUMPED BALLS. If the cue ball is jumped off the table (foul), it is spotted on the head spot (if occupied, the foot spot; if that is also occupied, the center spot).

If the white object ball is jumped, it is spotted on the head spot (if occupied, the foot spot; if that is also occupied, the center spot).

If the red object ball is jumped, it is spotted on the foot spot (if occupied, the head spot; if that is also occupied, the center spot). If the cue ball and an object ball are both jumped, the cue ball is spotted first, then the object ball following the appropriate spotting order above.

If both object balls are jumped, they are spotted as above. If the cue ball occupies either of the object balls' primary spot locations, spot first the ball that spots freely; then the other according to the appropriate alternative spotting order above.

Cushion Caroms

Except when clearly contradicted by these additional rules, the general rules of carom billiards apply.

PLAYERS. Two or three.

BALLS USED. Standard set of one white clear, one white spot, and one red.

OBJECT OF THE GAME. Score the predetermined number of points (may be thirty to sixty in tournament play, or any agreed upon number) for game prior to opponent(s).

SCORING. Each legal count is scored as one point for shooter.

DEFINITION OF A COUNT. A shot is a count if not in violation of any rules of play or general rules of carom billiards, and the cue ball contacts both object balls.

OPENING BREAK. General rules of carom billiards regarding opening break apply, as well as rule #2 below. Failure to comply is a violation; player's inning ends and no count can be scored.

RULES OF PLAY.

1. A legal counting stroke entitles shooter to continue at the table until he fails to legally count on a shot.

2. On all shots, player must cause the cue ball to either contact one or more cushions before contacting object balls, or contact an object ball directly and then one or more cushions before it contacts second object ball. Failure to comply is a violation; player's inning ends and no count can be scored on the violating stroke.

PENALTY FOR FOULS. One point is deducted from offender's score for each foul.

FOUR–BALL CAROMS

Except when clearly contradicted by these additional rules, the general rules of carom billiards apply.

PLAYERS. Two.

BALLS USED. Standard set of one white clear, one white spot and one red, plus one light red (pink).

OBJECT OF THE GAME. Score the predetermined number of points for game prior to opponent.

SCORING. Each legal two-ball-carom count is scored as one point for shooter; each legal three-ball carom count is scored as two points for shooter.

DEFINITION OF A COUNT. If not in violation of any rules of play or general rules of carom billiards, a shot is: A two-ball-carom count if the cue ball contacts any two of the three object balls, or a three-ball-carom count if the cue ball contacts all three of the object balls.

BALL POSITIONS—OPENING BREAK. The light red (pink) ball is spotted on the foot spot. The red ball is spotted on the head spot. Both balls are in position before the lag for break.

OPENING BREAK. The lag for break is actually part of the opening break with the red and pink balls spotted as immediately above. Players select cue balls and lag for break as in general rules of carom billiards (automatic loss of lag applying to contact with the pink ball as well as the red). When lag is completed, both players' cue balls remain in position; first shot of the game is from this position (if cue ball[s] contacted either red and/or pink object balls—which were spotted—on lag, they are re-spotted prior to first shot of game.). Winner of lag has choice of shooting first or assigning first shot to opponent; in either case, cue balls are played from position following lag for break, and each player's cue ball is the one he used for the lag for break. Starting player (first shooter after lag for break) must cause the cue ball's first contact with a ball to be with the pink object ball (on the foot spot). Failure to comply is a violation; player's inning ends and no count can be scored.

RULES OF PLAY.

1. On all shots subsequent to the first shot following the lag, shooter may make his first object (first ball contacted by the cue ball) any of the three object balls.

2. A legal counting stroke entitles shooter to continue at the table until he fails to legally count on a shot.

SPOTTING JUMPED BALLS. (Differs from general rules of carom billiards)

If the red ball is jumped off the table, it is spotted on the head spot. If the head spot is occupied (spotting a ball on it would result in contact with another ball), the red ball is held off the table until the first time the head spot is vacant at the completion of a shot.

If the pink ball is jumped, it is spotted on the foot spot. If the foot spot is occupied (spotting a ball on it would result in contact with another ball), the pink ball is held off the table until the first time the foot spot is vacant at the completion of a shot.

If the white object ball is jumped, it is spotted on the head spot. If the head spot is occupied, the white object ball is held off the table until the first time the head spot is vacant at the completion of a shot. Should the head spot be occupied after each shot until such time as the white object ball is required as incoming player's cue ball, that ball shall then be spotted on the foot spot; if the foot spot is also occupied, it shall be spotted on the center spot; if the center spot is also occupied, incoming player may place the ball anywhere on the head string, not frozen to a ball.

If the white cue ball is jumped, the same rule (immediately above) applies.

If the red ball and the pink balls are jumped on a shot, spot the pink ball first, then the red ball, according to spotting rules for those balls. If neither can be spotted per those rules, spot the pink ball on the center spot and continue holding the red ball off the table until the head spot is vacant per the red spotting-ball rule.

If either one of the white balls and one or both of the red balls are jumped on a shot, first spot of the white ball per appropriate rule above, then the red ball per appropriate rule (or if both reds, the immediately preceding paragraph).

If both of the white balls and one of the red balls is jumped, spot all balls that will spot directly (beginning with the white object ball, then the white cue ball, then the red). If all jumped balls cannot be spotted directly, spot remaining balls per appropriate rule above.

If all four balls are jumped on a shot, the jumper's cue ball is spotted on the center spot, the red ball on the head spot, and the pink on the foot spot, and the incoming player may place his cue ball anywhere on the head string not frozen to the red ball.

Jumped balls result in no penalty unless the player's cue ball is jumped. If player does jump his cue ball off the table, the stroke is invalid and is a foul.

PENALTY FOR FOULS.   One point is deducted from offender's score for each foul.

Straight Rail

Except when clearly contradicted by these additional rules, the general rules of carom billiards apply.

PLAYERS.   Two or three.

BALLS USED.   Standard set of one white clear, one white spot and one red.

OBJECT OF THE GAME.   Score the predetermined number of points for game prior to opponent(s).

SCORING.   Each legal count is scored as one point for shooter.

DEFINITION OF A COUNT.   A shot is a count if not in violation of any rules of play or general rules of carom billiards and the cue ball contacts both object balls.

OPENING BREAK.   General rules of carom billiards regarding opening break apply. Failure to comply is a violation; player's inning ends and no count can be scored.

RULES OF PLAY.

1. A legal counting stroke entitles shooter to continue at the table until he fails to legally count on a shot.

2. When the object balls are in a crotch, player may score no more than three successive counts with the balls remaining in the crotch. If three successive in-crotch counts are made, player must, on his next shot, drive at least one object ball out of the crotch. Failure to do is a violation; player's inning ends and no count can be scored.

PENALTY FOR FOULS. One point is deducted from offender's score for each foul.

United States Billiard Association Three—Cushion Rules

1. USBA sanctioned tournaments will be governed by the rules that follow. Any exception must be stated in the tournament notice, or discussed and approved by a majority of the players present before the start of any USBA tournament.

2. A three-cushion billiard is valid and is a count of one in any of the following cases: a) cue ball strikes an object ball and then strikes three or more cushions before striking the second object ball; b) cue ball strikes three or more cushions and then strikes the two object balls; c) cue ball strikes a cushion, then strikes one object ball, and then strikes two or more cushions before striking the second object ball; d) cue ball strikes two cushions, then strikes first object ball, and then strikes one or more cushions before striking the second object ball.

3. Three cushions means three impacts. The number of cushions does not mean three different ones; a valid count may be executed on one cushion, if they are the result of the overspin or underspin on the ball.

4. Lagging for the break. a) The two players select a cue ball, which is placed on the table within the head string, and stroke the ball to the foot of the table and return. The side rails may be touched by the ball in lagging, though it is not required. b) Player whose ball comes to rest nearest to the head rail wins the lag. c) The winner of the lag has the right to shoot the first shot or assign the break shot to the opponent. d) Winner of the lag has the choice of cue balls, which is then used for the duration of the game.

5. Break shot. a) Opponent's ball is placed on the head spot. Starting player's cue ball is placed within eight inches to the right or left of the head spot. Red ball is placed on the foot spot. b) Starting player must contact the red ball first. Failure to contact the red ball first is an error and ends the starting player's inning. c) On subsequent shots, either the red ball or cue ball can be the first object ball.

6. Fouls which end a player's turn. a) Jumped balls (see rule 11). b) Starting play while balls are in motion. c) Touching any of the balls by hand, part of clothing, cue or any other object such as chalk or pen. The balls shall remain in position to which they were thus moved. d) Push or shove shot (see rule 15). e) Double stroke (see rule 15). f) When, at moment of shooting, neither foot is touching the floor. g) Wrong ball (see rule 8). h) Touching ball with cue during warm-up (see rule 18). i) Player interference (see rule 20).

7. Any foul caused by outside interference is not to be charged as a penalty to the player with shot in progress. If the balls are displaced by the disturbance, they will be restored to their original position as precisely as possible, and the player will continue shooting.

8. Wrong ball. a) Shooting with the wrong ball is a foul and ends the player's inning. b) The opponent or the referee may call this foul; opponent may call before or after the shot, referee calls it only after the shot. c) Such a foul can be called at any time during a run, but the shooter shall be entitled to all points made previous to the stroke in which error was detected. d) The incoming shooter shall play the balls as left after error was called.

9. Frozen balls. a) If during the course of an inning the shooter's ball comes to rest in contact with the opponent's ball, the shooter has the option of playing away from the ball with which he is in contact or electing to have the balls in contact spotted. b) If an inning ends with the shooter's ball in contact with the next shooter's ball, or the red ball in contact with the next shooter's ball, the incoming player has the option of playing away from the ball in contact or may elect to have the two balls which are in contact spotted. c) Only those balls which are in contact are to be spotted. The loose or unfrozen ball is not to be touched. The red ball is spotted on the foot spot, the player's cue ball on the head spot, and the opponent's cue ball on the center spot. d) If the spot reserved for the ball to be spotted is hidden by another ball, the ball to be spotted is placed on the spot usually reserved for the hiding ball. e) The same rules apply when a ball or balls jump the table.

10. When a cue ball is frozen to a cushion, a player may shoot into (play against) that cushion, but the first contact shall not count. Subsequent contacts with the same cushion are valid.

11. When a player's cue ball, the opponent's ball, or the red ball jumps the table, it is a foul and the player's inning ends. Spot balls as per rule #9 (c,d).

12. No shot can be started while balls are still in motion, or are still spinning. If a player disregards this rule, it is a foul and inning ends.

13. When the cue ball bounces and rides the top of the rail and returns to the table, the ball is in play. It shall count as one cushion. If it rides two or more rails, each rail will count as a cushion. If ball remains on top of the rail, it is considered a jumped ball, which is a foul, and player's inning ends.

14. If in playing a shot the cue ball leaves the playing surface and rides the rail or cushion, regardless of the number of impacts on that cushion, only one impact will be allowed.

15. If a player has pushed or shoved the cue ball with his cue, it is a foul and player's inning ends. A push shot is one in which the cue tip remains in contact with the cue ball after cue ball strikes an object ball, or when cue tip again contacts the cue ball after cue ball strikes the object ball. Double stroke occurs when player's tip or cue shaft hits cue ball twice. If a billiard is made, it shall not count, and the player's inning ends.

16. All kiss shots are fair, whether they deprive a player of an imminent score, or whether they assist in a score.

17. Miscues shall not end the player's inning, unless it is construed that the player's ferrule or shaft also touched the cue ball. Not all miscues are fouls, and if a billiard is completed in the miscue stroke, it shall be counted and turn continues.

18. If a player during the "warm-up" stroking should touch the cue ball, it is a foul and inning ends.

19. A game is official when a player scores the number of points constituting a game, even though the opponent has had one less turn at the table. If a scorekeeper is used, the game becomes official after the score sheet is signed by the players. The referee and the scorekeeper should also sign the sheet. After the losing player signs the score sheet, no protest can be made.

20. If a player at the table is responsible for interference in any manner, it is a foul, and the inning ends. Incoming player must accept balls in position. A player not at the table must not distract the opponent with undue motions or noise. The referee or tournament official may issue a warning or disqualify the player for unsportsmanlike conduct.

21. If, for reasons beyond his control, a player cannot start a game as scheduled, the game may be postponed if the tournament director so decides. If a player is unable to finish a game, he forfeits the game, unless the opponent waives the forfeiture and agrees to finish the game at a time convenient to the tournament management. If a player is unable to return to the tournament, all his games are nullified as they would be in disqualification.

22. If a player is disqualified in a game, he loses that game and gets no points. The opponent is credited with a game won and is given the number of points he would have scored had he won the game. If a player is disqualified from a tournament, all his games are nullified (games played and games remaining on the schedule). Tournament continues as though one less player started when tournament opened.

23. If, for reasons beyond his control, a player cannot start a game, he must notify the tournament manager in time to allow for a substitute player, or for another pair of players. All tournament contestants are subject to immediate call if a substitute is necessary.

24. If a referee is officiating and considers a player to be taking an abnormal amount of time between strokes or in determining the choice of shots with the intention of upsetting his opponent, the referee shall warn the player that he runs the risk of disqualification if he pursues these tactics. Continued disregard of the warning shall be proper grounds to disqualify the player. If no referee is officiating, the tournament manager shall have the right to invoke this rule.

25. Deliberate safeties are not allowed. If played, the incoming player may accept balls as they are, or set up a break shot.

26. At any tournament sanctioned by the USBA, the tournament director plus some other member of the USBA who is not playing in the tournament shall constitute a grievance committee to whom unsportsmanlike conduct during the tournament may be reported. Before commencement of the tournament, the players shall designate two of the players to serve on such a committee to protect the interests of the players. The two persons representing the USBA and the two persons representing the players shall jointly consider any evidence or reports of unsportsmanlike conduct. If this grievance committee is unable to resolve the complaint, the representatives shall submit a written report to the USBA for consideration by the Board of Directors. The two player representatives may indicate their concurrence in the findings of the USBA representatives or may submit dissenting views to the Board of Directors. At the next regular meeting or special meeting of the Board of Directors, these reports shall be considered and the action recommended by a majority shall be binding on the accused member of the USBA.

THE DIAMOND SYSTEM

There are various systems in billiards that make use of the spots, or diamonds, inset in the rails. Numerical values assigned to the diamonds enable players to plan shots, particularly bank shots, with the help of simple arithmetic. Some world-class players don't use diamond systems, some use them only to check their instinct or judgment, some use them at every opportunity. The fact is, on many shots in three-cushion billiards, diamond systems greatly reduce the need for guesswork. What follows is a description of the most widely used system, the "corner 5," also called "the diamond system," or simply "the system."

A cue ball hit with slight running English that strikes the third rail at diamond no. 1 will travel back to diamond no. 7 on the first cushion. If it strikes diamond no. 2 on the third rail it will travel back to diamond no. 8 on the first rail (or corner). Diamond no. 3 on the third rail connects with diamond no. 3 (object-ball number) on the lower rail. The various diamonds connect as illustrated in Figure 12–1. A player must memorize these connections to use the diamond system, since he must know the path the ball will travel after it comes off the third rail.

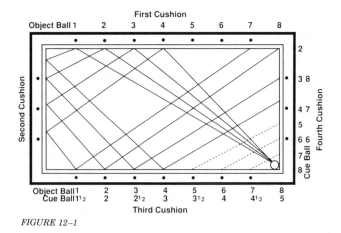

FIGURE 12–1

Playing the diamond system, the player studies his shot backward—that is, he must find out where he will come off the third cushion to score. Say, for example, that both object balls lie in the upper-right corner of Figure 12-1 with the cue ball in the lower-right corner as shown.

The player, having memorized the connecting diamonds, knows that he must come off diamond no. 2 on the third rail to bank the shot in that corner.

Note that there are object-ball markings on the third cushion. They start from no. 1 at the first diamond and go down to 8, which is the corner. If the player has to come off the second diamond, his object-ball number is 2.

Note there are cue-ball numbers on the third cushion. They start with 1½ on the first diamond and go down to 5, which is the corner. The cue-ball numbers also continue on the lower rail, as 6, 7, and 8. (See Fig. 12-1).

The player is still playing the bank shot with the two object balls in the lower right-hand corner. He knows up to this time that he must come off diamond no. 2 on the third rail to count.

He must figure out where he will hit on the first cushion to bring his cue ball back to diamond no. 2 on the third cushion. In the figure the cue ball lies at cue ball no. 5, which is the corner. Thus, knowing the object-ball number (2) and the cue-ball number (5), he subtracts the object-ball number (2) from the cue-ball number (5) and gets 3, which is the diamond he must hit on the first rail. If he wants to get to diamond no. 1 on the third rail, with the cue ball still at 5, he subtracts 1 from 5 and gets 4, the diamond he must hit on the first rail. If he wants to get to 3 on the third rail, he subtracts 3 from 5 and gets 2.

If he wants to get to 2 on the third rail and finds the cue ball is at 6 on the lower rail, he subtracts 2 from 6 and gets 4, which is where he will hit on the first rail. If the cue ball lies at 3½ as a cue ball number and he wants to get to 2 on the third rail, he subtracts 2 from 3½ and gets 1½, which he must hit on the first rail.

Note that when a ball lies at cue-ball position no. 5 (see Fig. 12-1) and the player is playing to come off the cushion at 2 on the third rail, player must hit 3 on the first cushion. The figure shows a line running from cue-ball position 5 to the 3 diamond on the first cushion.

That line is cue-ball position 5, no matter where the cue ball rests on that line. If the ball is in the corner it is 5. If the cue ball is on the line and four inches from the first cushion, it is still cue-ball number 5.

Our discussion to this point covers only bank shots. The system can also be used when a ball is hit first. Consider the position in Figure 12-2. In shots of this type, the first object ball gives the player his cue-ball number. Suppose the first object ball lies on the line of cue-ball position 5, as we discussed immediately above. If the player drove the object ball on cue-ball line 5 into the first cushion at diamond no. 3, he would hit the third cushion at 2 and travel to the

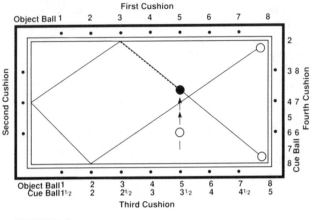

FIGURE 12–2

lower right-hand corner, assuming the second object ball is in that corner.

However, the player cannot drive the object ball with his cue. So, knowing the first object ball rests on cue-ball line 5, he must drive the cue ball from the first object ball into the first cushion at diamond no. 3 to come off the third rail at diamond no. 2 and make the shot on the second object ball in the lower right-hand corner. Here, the ability to make caroms reveals its importance.

The most important thing in three-cushion billiards is being able to drive the cue ball from the first object ball into the first cushion at the point desired. In other words, unless the player can make the simple carom of driving the cue ball from the first object ball into the desired point of the first cushion, his chances of making the count are minimized.

If the first object ball lies on cue-ball track (or line) 4½ and the player wants to come off diamond no. 2 on the third cushion, he subtracts 2 from 4½ and then proceeds to drive his cue ball off the first object ball into 2½ on the first cushion (which is 2 from 4½).

Many players refuse to learn the diamond system, because written explanations of it are somewhat complicated and require studious attention. However, if the player will follow the instructions above and test them out on a table, he will find the system is comparatively simple. Oral explanations from a player who knows the system make for easier understanding, of course.

The diamond system is not infallible, but on bank shots particularly it serves a player better than his instinct. If you watch a player in world tournament as he studies a bank shot, he will determine first from what point he must come off the third rail to score.

Say he has to come off diamond 2½ on the third rail. He then determines his cue-ball number. Say it is 4½. By subtracting 2½ from 4½ he knows he must hit diamond no. 2 on the first rail to get back to diamond no. 2½ on the third rail. The system tells him exactly where to hit. His instinct may have given him the general location of the desired point on the first cushion, but if he hit 1¾ or 2¼ on the first rail, chances are he would miss the shot.

When using the diamond system, strike the cue ball above center with running English, following through on your stroke. If you stab the cue ball with a jerky stroke you will shorten the angle. If you slam the cue ball too hard you are likely to shorten the angle. Use a stroke of medium force and follow through.

If the balls do not lie exactly on the object-ball and cue-ball tracks, you may parallel or you may figure the diamonds in fractions. For example, if the object-ball number is 1¼ and the cue-ball number is 3½, your subtraction gives you point 2¼ on the first rail. The diamond system does not apply to all shots on the table. It is confined almost entirely to natural-angle shots.

You may find that in using the diamond system on a certain table that your cue ball "comes short." If this happens, you allow for it in your calculations, moving up higher on the first rail. Thus, instead of hitting 2 (assuming your calculations tell you to hit 2) you move up to 1¾ or maybe 1½. Make sure first, however, that you are stroking your cue ball with running English and are following through before you decide the table runs short.

When using the diamond system, aim at the diamond through the cushion—that is, at an angle through the cushion to the diamond, which is set back on the rail. Do not aim at a point at the edge of the cushion which is directly opposite the diamond.

THREE-CUSHION PRACTICE SHOTS

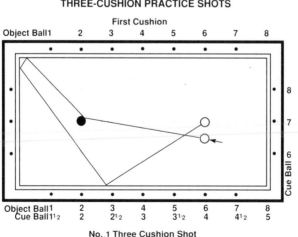

THREE-CUSHION PRACTICE SHOTS

No..1 Three Cushion Shot

FIGURE 12–3 Hold cue level. Hit object ball ⅓ right. Strike cue ball center, slight English left. Use seven-inch bridge. Employ moderate stroke.

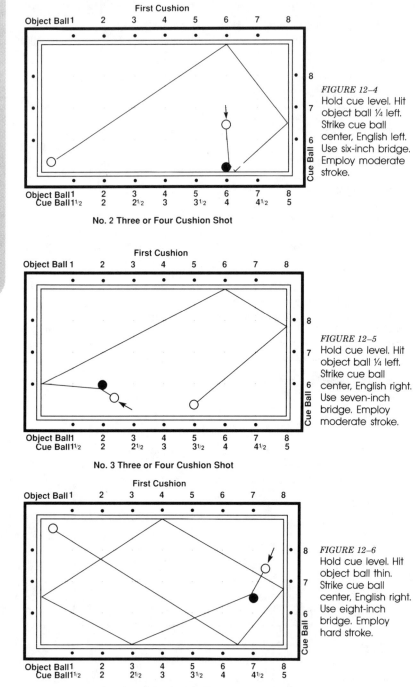

First Cushion

Object Ball 1 2 3 4 5 6 7 8

8
7
6 Cue Ball

FIGURE 12–4
Hold cue level. Hit object ball ¼ left. Strike cue ball center, English left. Use six-inch bridge. Employ moderate stroke.

Object Ball	1	2	3	4	5	6	7	8
Cue Ball	1½	2	2½	3	3½	4	4½	5

No. 2 Three or Four Cushion Shot

First Cushion

Object Ball 1 2 3 4 5 6 7 8

8
7
6 Cue Ball

FIGURE 12–5
Hold cue level. Hit object ball ¼ left. Strike cue ball center, English right. Use seven-inch bridge. Employ moderate stroke.

Object Ball	1	2	3	4	5	6	7	8
Cue Ball	1½	2	2½	3	3½	4	4½	5

No. 3 Three or Four Cushion Shot

First Cushion

Object Ball 1 2 3 4 5 6 7 8

8
7
6 Cue Ball

FIGURE 12–6
Hold cue level. Hit object ball thin. Strike cue ball center, English right. Use eight-inch bridge. Employ hard stroke.

Object Ball	1	2	3	4	5	6	7	8
Cue Ball	1½	2	2½	3	3½	4	4½	5

No. 4 Five or Six Cushion Shot

TOURNAMENT RESULTS AND RECORDS

For records of tournaments no longer held, check the listings at the back of this section first and then prior editions of the BCA Official Rules and Record Book.

BCA NATIONAL INDIVIDUAL EIGHT-BALL CHAMPIONS

Men's Division

1977–Tom Kilburn, Dayton, OH, ... Runner-up–Dick Spitzer
1978–Mike Carella, Louisville, KY, ... Runner-up–Bob Williams
1979–Jimmy Reid, Louisville, KY, ... Runner-up–Mark Wilson
1980–Nick Varner, Columbus, OH, ... Runner-up–Mike Massey
1981–Danny DiLiberto, Las Vegas, NV, ... Runner-up–Nick Varner
1982–Joe Sposit, Kansas City, MO, ... Runner-up–Gregg Fix
1983–Michael Sardelli, Detroit, MI, ... Runner-up–Tom Chapman
1984–Louie Lemke, Fort Worth, TX, ... Runner-up–Charles Shotman
1985–Steve Matlock, Cedar Rapids, IA, ... Runner-up–Stan Fimple
1986–Jesus Rivera, Denver, CO, ... Runner-up–Mickey Leon Stone
1987–Stan Fimple, Omaha, NE, ... Runner-up–Mike Fenne
1988–Harry Sexton, Detroit, MI, ... Runner-up–Seco Varani
1989–Henry Granas, Englewood, CO, ... Runner-up–T. J. Davis
1990–Jesus Rivera, Denver, CO, ... Runner-up–Gilbert Martinez
1991–Paul Guernsey, Plano, TX, ... Runner-up–Gene Rossi

Women's Division

1978–Catherine Stephens, Louisville, KY, ... Runner-up–Melodie Horn
1979–Gloria Walker, Louisville, KY, ... Runner-up–Mary Kenniston
1980–Billie Billing, Columbus, OH, ... Runner-up–Gloria Walker
1981–Belinda Campos, Las Vegas, NV, ... Runner-up–Sherry Lively
1982–Linda Hoffman, Kansas City, MO, ... Runner-up–Sherry Lively
1983–Georgina Casteel, Detroit, MI, ... Runner-up–Sherry Lively
1984–Belinda Campos Bearden, Fort Worth, TX, .. Runner-up–Linda Hoffman
1985–Linda Hoffman, Arlington, TX, ... Runner-up–Diane Piercy
1986–Linda Hoffman, Arlington, TX, ... Runner-up–Christine Glass
1987–Linda Hoffman, Arlington, TX, ... Runner-up–Janene Hague
1988–Timi Bloomberg, Rapid City, SD, ... Runner-up–Kathy Miao
1989–Sherry Lively, Carmichael, CA, ... Runner-up–Christine Glass
1990–Linda Meyer, Ponca City, OK, ... Runner-up–Janene Hague
1991–Suzi Quall, Appleton, WI, ... Runner-up–Chris Fields

Senior Men's Division

1986–Stanley Coscia, Tampa, FL, ... Runner-up–Harold Schnormeier
1987–Jerry Priest, Cape Girardeau, MO, ... Runner-up–Bob Keating
1988–Seco Varani, Faribault, MN, ... Runner-up–Bob Keating
1989–Jerry Priest, Cape Girardeau, MO, ... Runner-up–Bob Vanover

1990–Jerry Priest, Cape Girardeau, MO, ... Runner-up–Bernard Rogoff
1991–Bob Vanover, Dallas, TX, ... Runner-up–Beau Zimmerman
1992–Seco Varani, Faribault, MN, ... Runner-up—Fred Guarino

Senior Women's Division
1989–Fern Reedy, Smithville, MO, ... Runner-up–Jeanne Bloomberg
1990–Jeri Engh, Osceola, WI, ... Runner-up–Op Wheeler
1991–Karen Wold, St. Paul, MN, ... Runner-up–Lynn Reed
1992–Lynn Reed, New Berlin, WI, ... Runner-up–Charlene Edwards

SCOTCH-DOUBLES DIVISION
1991 . . . . Bonnie and Mark Coats (Broken Arrow, OK)
1992 . . . . Janey Finn and Pete Lewis (Clinton, IA)

BCA NATIONAL 8-BALL TEAM CHAMPIONS
Master Men
1991 . . . . Black Sticks (Houston, TX)
1992 . . . . The Crunch Bunch (Dallas, TX)

Women
1979 . . . . . . Wheel Inn (Billings, MT)
1980 . . . . Burt's Girls (Colorado Springs, CO)
1981 . . . . Burt's Girls (Colorado Springs, CO)
1982 . . . . Richard's (Lansing, MI)
1983 . . . . Richard's (Lansing, MI)
1984 . . . North Star (Sacramento, CA)
1985 . . . Gold Nugget (Arlington, TX)
1986 . . . . Leisure Club (Phoenix, AZ)
1987 . . . . . Leftys + (Sacramento, CA)
1988 . . . . Great American Girls (Sacramento, CA)
1989 8-Ball Express (Rapid City, SD)
1990 8-Ball Express (Rapid City, SD)
1991 . . . . Cue-Ts (West Allis, WI)
1992 . . Lucky Ladies (Ft. Worth, TX)

Men
1979 . . . . . . Tam O'Shanter (Colorado Springs, CO)
1980 . . . . . . Tam O'Shanter (Colorado Springs, CO)
1981 . . . . . . Tam O'Shanter (Colorado Springs, CO)
1982 . . . . The Wizards (Colorado Springs, CO)
1983 . Mike's Lounge (Pittsburgh, PA)
1984 . . . Green Acres (Ft. Worth, TX)
1985 Starlite Lounge (Arlington, TX)
1986 . . . . . . MeMaws (Ft. Worth, TX)
1987 . . . . . . Jackson All Stars (Grand Prairie, TX)
1988 . . . . . . Mongo Murph's (Windsor, Canada)
1989 . . . . Black Sticks (Houston, TX)
1990 . . . . Black Sticks (Houston, TX)
1991 . . . . Players (San Antonio, TX)
1992 . . . . Lassiters (Clinton, IA

BCA NATIONAL JUNIOR EIGHT-BALL CHAMPIONS
1989–Chan Whitt, Jr., Lewisburg, WV, ... Runner-up–Chad Duster
1990–Nathan Haddad, Lansing, MI (15–18 division) Runner-up–Scott Marshall
    –Michael Coltrain, Raleigh, NC (14 and under) Runner-up–Chris Whitten
1991–Max Eberle, Arlington, VA (15–18 division) . . . . Runner-up–Chan Whitt
    –Charles Williams, Newport News, VA (14 and under) . . Runner-up–Kelsey Jorgensen
1992–Mike Rinella, Abington, MA (15–18 division) Runner-up–Larry Nevel, Jr.
    –Andy Quinn, St. Charles, MO (14 and under) Runner-up–Jesse Bowman

ACU-I POCKET BILLIARD CHAMPIONS (MEN)
1937 . . . . . John O. Miller . . . . University of Wisconsin
1938 . . . . . J. L. Geiger . . . . University of Florida
1939 . . . . Peter Choulas . . . . Colgate University
1940 . . . . . John O. Miller . . . . University of Wisconsin

1941	Lloyd Green	University of Kansas
1942	Leo Bonimi	Cornell University
1943	Leff Mabie	University of Florida
1944	J. Zvanya	University of Indiana
1945–46	(No Tournament)	
1947	Leff Mabie	University of Florida
1948	Jack Brown	University of Utah
1949	Leroy Kinman	Eastern Kentucky State
1950	Leroy Kinman	Eastern Kentucky State
1951	Leroy Kinman	Eastern Kentucky State
1952	Bill Simms	University of Georgia
1953	John Beaudette	Michigan State College
1954	John Beaudette	Michigan State College
1955	Rodney Boyd	Ohio State University
1956	Joseph Sapanaro	Suffolk University
1957	Joseph Sapanaro	Suffolk University
1958	Lloyd Courter	State University of Iowa
1959	Donald Dull	State College of Washington
1960	Henry Parks	Indiana University
1961	Jim Finucane	University of Notre Dame
1962	Robert Burke	University of Oregon
1963	Larry Galloway	Indiana University
1964	William Hendricks	Southern Illinois University
1965	William Wells	Tulane University
1966	William Wells	Tulane University
1967	Richard Baumgarth	Purdue University
1968	Marshall Boelter	Univ. of Illinois, Chicago Circle Campus
1969	Nick Varner	Purdue University
1970	Nick Varner	Purdue University
1971	Keith Woestehoff	Ohio University
1972	Andrew Tennent	University of Wisconsin
1973	Dan Louie	Washington State University
1974	Dan Louie	Washington State University
1975	Robert Jewett	University of California–Berkeley
1976	John Cianflone	Rutgers University
1977	Jay Hungerford	Arizona State University
1978	Steve Cusick	University of Illinois–Urbana
1979	Peter Lhotka	University of North Dakota
1980	Rob Havick	University of Minnesota–Duluth
1981	(No Tournament)	
1982	Thomas Golly	Penn State University
1983	Robert Madenjian	Kansas State University
1984	Gary French	California State College–Stanislaus
1985	(No Tournament)	
1986	Gary Asbell	Florida State University
1987	Bill Beardsley	University of Michigan
1988	Nick Kucharew	Mohawk College
1989	Gary Asbell	Florida State University
1990	Marc Oelslager	St. Cloud State University
1991	Frank Alonso	University of Nebraska–Lincoln
1992	David Uwate	University of Florida

ACU-I POCKET BILLIARD CHAMPIONS (WOMEN)

1929	Margaret Anderson	University of Illinois
1942	Emily Ann Julian	South Dakota State College
1943	Mary Jean Noonan	South Dakota State College
1944	Barbara Jackson	Colorado State College of Ed.

1948	Jeanne Lynch	Rhode Island State
1949	Cora Libbey	University of Wisconsin
1950	(No Tournament)	
1951	Ramona Fielder	South Dakota State College
1952	Sonda Bilsky	Purdue University
1953	Joanne Skonning	Purdue University
	Jackie Slusher	Oregon State College
1954	Lee McGary	University of Oregon
1955	Judy Ferles	University of Arizona
1956	Judy Ferles	University of Arizona
1957	No Coed Face to Face	
1958	No Coed Face to Face	
1959	Jan Deeter	Purdue University
1960	Darlene McCabe	University of Oregon
1961	Ann Sidlauskas	Indiana University
1962	San Merrick	Bowling Green State University
1963	Barbara Watkins	Bowling Green State University
1964	Barbara Watkins	Bowling Green State University
1965	Susan Sloan	University of Texas
1966	Linda Randolph	Iowa State University
1967	Shirley Glicen	University of Miami
1968	Gail Allums	University of Iowa
1969	Donna Ries	University of Missouri at Kansas City
1970	Catherine Stephens	Western Washington State
1971	Marcia Girolamo	State Univ. of New York at Oswego
1972	Krista Hartmann	Sante Fe Community College, Gainesville, Florida
1973	Marcia Girolamo	State University of New York at Oswego
1974	Janice Ogawa	Boise State University
1975	Debra Weiner	Northern Illinois University
1976	Melissa Rice	University of Wisconsin–Milwaukee
1977	Julie Bentz	University of Wisconsin–Madison
1978	Mari Dana Heydon	Oregon State University
1979	Julie Bentz Fitzpatrick	University of Wisconsin–Madison
1980	Shari Verrill	University of Wisconsin–Madison
1981	(No Tournament)	
1982	Jane Bartram	University of Colorado
1983	Helen Yamasaki	California State University–LA
1984	Shirley Weathers	Triton College
1985	(No Tournament)	
1986	Kathy Trabue	Ohio State University
1987	Penny Beile	University of Kentucky
1988	Janet Dordell	Penn State University
1989	Cathy Petrowski	North Texas State University
1990	Susan Tillotson	Florida State University
1991	Leanne Okada	University of California–Berkeley
1992	Laura Bendikas	University of Illinois–Urbana

BCA'S U.S. OPEN 14.1 POCKET-BILLIARD CHAMPIONSHIP RECORDS

Men's Division

Irving Crane 1966, Chicago, IL	Runner-up–Joe Balsis
Jimmy Caras 1967, St. Louis, MO	Runner-up–Luther Lassiter
Joe Balsis 1968, Lansing, MI	Runner-up–Danny DiLiberto
Luther Lassiter 1969, Las Vegas, NV	Runner-up–Jack Breit
Steve Mizerak 1970, Chicago, IL	Runner-up–Luther Lassiter
Steve Mizerak 1971, Chicago, IL	Runner-up–Joe Balsis
Steve Mizerak 1972, Chicago, IL	Runner-up–Dan DiLiberto

Steve Mizerak 1973, Chicago, IL .... Runner-up–Luther Lassiter
Joe Balsis 1974, Chicago, IL .... Runner-up–Jim Rempe
Dallas West 1975, Chicago, IL .... Runner-up–Pete Margo
Tom Jennings 1976, Chicago, IL .... Runner-up–Joe Balsis
Tom Jennings 1977, Dayton, OH .... Runner-up–Richard Lane
Dallas West 1983, Detroit, MI .... Runner-up–Nick Varner
Oliver Ortmann 1989, Chicago, IL .... Runner-up–Steve Mizerak
Mike Sigel 1992, New York, NY .... Runner-up–Dallas West

Women's Division

Dorothy Wise 1967, St. Louis, MO .... Runner-up–San Lynn Merrick
Dorothy Wise 1968, Lansing, MI .... Runner-up–San Lynn Merrick
Dorothy Wise 1969, Las Vegas, NV .... Runner-up–San Lynn Merrick
Dorothy Wise 1970, Chicago, IL .... Runner-up–Sheila Bohm
Dorothy Wise 1971, Chicago, IL .... Runner-up–Geraldine Titcomb
Jean Balukas 1972, Chicago, IL .... Runner-up–Madelyn Whitlow
Jean Balukas 1973, Chicago, IL .... Runner-up–Donna Ries
Jean Balukas 1974, Chicago, IL .... Runner-up–Mieko Harada
Jean Balukas 1975, Chicago, IL .... Runner-up–Mieko Harada
Jean Balukas 1976, Chicago, IL .... Runner-up–Gloria Walker
Jean Balukas 1977, Dayton, OH .... Runner-up–Gloria Walker
Jean Balukas 1983, Detroit, MI .... Runner-up–Loree Jon Ogonowski
Loree Jon Jones 1989, Chicago, IL .... Runner-up–Robin Bell
Loree Jon Jones 1992, New York, NY .... Runner-up–Ewa Mataya

U.S. OPEN RECORDS—1966–1992

Men's Division

High run in the money: 150 by Irving Crane (vs. Joe Balsis), 1966/150 by Mike Sigel (vs. Jim Rempe), 1989/150 by Mike Sigel (vs. Mike Zaglan), 1992/150 by Johnny Archer (vs. Jeff Carter), 1992.

High run out of the money: 116 by Rodney "Babe" Thompson, 1972.

High BPI average, tournament18.66 by Steve Mizerak, 1972.

Most championships won: 4 by Steve Mizerak; 1970–1973 inclusive.

Most consecutive championships won: 4 by Steve Mizerak, 1970–1973 inclusive.

Most runner-up finishes: 3 by Balsis (1966, 1971, 1976) and Lassiter (1967, 1970, 1973).

Greatest victory margin (150-point match): 163 by Dick Baertsch (vs. Balsis), 1969.

Most games won, career: 57 by Dallas West (1966–1992 inclusive).

Best winning percentage, tournament: 1.000 by Crane, 1966; Mizerak, 1971; West, 1975, Sigel, 1992.

Fewest innings by champion (32-man field): 53 by Steve Mizerak, 1972.

Most consecutive match victories: 12 by Steve Mizerak (1970–1972).

Most high run awards: 3 by West (1966, 1967, 1976) and Balsis (1968, 1969, 1973).

Best game (150 points): 1 inning by Mike Sigel (vs. Mike Zuglen), 1989.

Best game (200 points): 16 innings by Joe Balsis (vs. J. Rempe), 1974.

Most appearances, career: 15 by Dallas West (1966–1992 inclusive).

U.S. OPEN RECORDS—1967–1992

Women's Division

High run in the money: 68 by Ewa Mataya (vs. Cathy Vanover), 1992.

High run out of the money: 28 by Jean Ann (Williams) Cardwell, 1967.

Most runner-up finishes: 2 by San Lynn Merrick, Gerry Titcomb and Mieko Harada.

Most consecutive match victories: 37 by Jean Balukas (1972–1983 inclusive).

High BPI average, tournament: 5.18 by Loree Jon Jones, 1989.

Most games won, career: 43 by Jean Balukas.

Best winning percentage, tournament: 1.000 by Wise (67–68, 70–71) and Balukas (72–83).

Best winning percentage, career (minimum 3 Opens or 10 games): .850 by Jean Balukas.

Most championships won: 7 by Jean Balukas; 1972–1983.

Most consecutive championships won: 7 by Jean Balukas; 1972–1983 inclusive.

Most high run awards: 5 by Balukas (72, 73, 75, 77, 83).

Best game (75 points): 3 innings by Jean Balukas (vs. Belinda Campos), 1977.

Best game (100 points): 13 innings by Loree Jon Jones (vs. Gerry Titcomb and vs. Belinda Bearden), 1989/13 innings by Robin Bell (vs. Gloria Walker), 1989/13 innings by Mary Kenniston (vs. Nesli O'Hare) 1992.

Best game (125 points): 13 innings by Loree Jon Jones (vs. Robin Bell), 1989.

Most appearances, career: 11 by Gerry Titcomb (1967–1989 inclusive).

BILLIARD FEDERATION OF U.S.A. CHAMPIONS

1968	Allen Gilbert	1979	Eddie Robin
1969	Bill Hynes	1980	Harry Sims
1970	Allen Gilbert	1981	George Ashby
1971	Allen Gilbert	1982	Carlos Hallon
1972	Eddie Robin	1983	Harry Sims
1973	John Bonner	1984	George Ashby
1974	Frank Torres	1985	Frank Torres
1975	John Bonner	1986	Carlos Hallon (held in March '86)
1976	George Ashby		
1977	Allen Gilbert	1987	Allen Gilbert
1978	Frank Torres	1988	Allen Gilbert

AMERICAN BILLIARDS ASSOCIATION

1969	Bud Harris		Allen Gilbert .. Western
1970	Bud Harris	1984 ...	Carlos Hallon .. Eastern
1971	Jim Cattrano		George Ashby .. Central
1972	Jim Cattrano		not held .... Western
1973	Allen Gilberg	1985 ...	3 tied for 1st ... Eastern
1974	not held		Ira Goldberg
1975	George Ashby		Bill Maloney
1976	Allen Gilbert		Dick Reid
1977	Allen Gilbert		George Ashby .. Central
1978	George Ashby		Rick Bryck ..... Western
1979	George Ashby	1986 ...	Dick Reid ...... Eastern
1980	George Ashby		Bill Smith ...... Central
Changed to 3 Regionals			Nahib Yousri ... Western
1981 ...	Carlos Hallon .. Eastern	1987 ...	Dick Reid ...... Eastern
	George Ashby .. Central		George Ashby .. Central
	Allen Gilbert .. Western		Harry Sims .... Western
1982 ...	Chris Bartzos .. Eastern	1988 ...	Carlos Hallon .. Eastern
	Bill Hawkins ... Central		Mike Donnelly .. Central
	Allen Gilbert .. Western		Allen Gilbert .. Western
1983 ...	Dick Reid ...... Eastern		
	George Ashby .. Central		

In September 1988, the BFUSA and ABA merged to form the USBA.

USBA NATIONALS

1989	Carlos Hallon
1990	Sang Lee
1991	Sang Lee

MEN'S POCKET-BILLIARD CHAMPIONS 1878–1991

*Compiled by Charles Ursitti, Mike Shamos
and Ken Shouler*

The game of pocket billiards in the United States evolved slowly beginning in the 1830s. The present competitive form, known as straight pool or 14.1 continuous, was not invented until 1910 and did not become the official championship game until 1921, when the term pocket billiards was first introduced. The earliest championship game was called "61-pool," a single-rack game with fifteen numbered object balls. Each ball was worth a number of points equal to its numerical value; the first player to score at least sixty-one points was the winner. A match consisted of a race to a certain number of games, usually twenty-one. This was the game played for the championship from 1878 until 1888.

Because a ball in 61-pool can be worth from one to fifteen points, it was possible to win a match by sinking far fewer balls than one's opponent. This unfairness was corrected in 1889, when the game of continuous pool was introduced. The players still played individual fifteen-ball racks without a break ball, but each ball counted for only one point and the first player to reach a predetermined point total, usually 100, was the winner. The player who sank the last ball of a rack would break the full pack on the next rack. No ball had to be called on the break, so it was possible for long runs to occur extending over many racks. The record run at continuous pool is still ninety-six, achieved by Alfredo De Oro in a nonchampionship game in 1911.

The break shot in continuous pool was very risky, since it is difficult to sink a ball in a controlled fashion when hitting a full rack of fifteen balls. Top players tended to play safety at the end of a rack rather than miss with the balls spread. This caused title games to become boring, as the audience could look forward to an exchange of safeties every fifteen balls. To eliminate the problem, Jerome Keogh, the champion in 1910 and teacher of future champion Irving Crane, suggested that the last ball of each rack be left free to be used as a target on the next rack. He proposed the name, "14-racked, 1 ball free," which became 14.1 continuous. It was adopted as the championship form for the tournament of April, 1912, won by Edward Ralph, who thus became the first straight-pool champion.

At first, championships were established by donors, such as the Brunswick-Balke-Collender Corporation. These expired after a certain time and new tournament had to be held to determine the next champion. In between tournaments, the champion was obliged to defend the title against challengers, who would meet the champion in a two-man match. Until the 1940s, this was the dominant method by which the title was decided, much as in boxing. It is therefore incorrect in most cases to associate a single champion with a particular year. Not all tournaments advertised as for the title are listed, but only those that were sanctioned by an appropriate governing body.

The table listed below lists all 206 times that the pocket-billiard title has changed hands or become vacant. The date listed is the month in which the title change occurred. (In some cases, tournaments or matches took place over a period of many months lasting as long as a baseball season.) The "champion" is the name of the titleholder. "Runner-up" indicates the player who lost the title match, or, in the case of a tournament, the player finishing in second place. From 1878 through 1888, the game was 61-pool. Continuous pool was the championship game from 1889 to 1911. Straight pool has been the championship game since 1912.

Apr, 1878–Cyrille Dion .... Runner-Up–Samuel F. Knight
Aug, 1878–Gotthard Walhstrom .... Runner-Up–Cyrille Dion
Apr, 1879–Samuel F. Knight .... Runner-Up–Gotthard Walhstrom
Aug, 1879–Alonzo Morris .... Runner-Up–Samuel F. Knight
Oct, 1879–Gotthard Walhstrom .... Runner-Up–Alonzo Morris
Feb, 1880–Samuel F. Knight .... Runner-Up–Gotthard Walhstrom
May 1880–Gotthard Walhstrom .... Runner-Up–Samuel F. Knight
Jan, 1881–Gotthard Walhstrom .... Runner-Up–Albert M. Frey
Jun, 1881–Gotthard Walhstrom .... Runner-Up–Albert M. Frey
Jan, 1884–James L. Malone .. Runner-Up–Albert M. Frey, Joseph T. King (tie)
Mar, 1886–Albert M. Frey .... Runner-Up–James L. Malone
May, 1886–Albert M. Frey .... Runner-Up–James L. Malone
Feb, 1887–Albert M. Frey .... Runner-Up–James L. Malone
Apr, 1887–Albert M. Frey .... Runner-Up–James L. Malone
May, 1887–James L. Malone .... Runner-Up–Albert M. Frey
May, 1887–Alfredo De Oro .... Runner-Up–James L. Malone
Feb, 1888–Alfredo De Oro .... Runner-Up–James L. Malone
Mar, 1889–Albert M. Frey .... Runner-Up–Alfredo De Oro
Apr, 1889–Title vacant (Frey died)
June, 1889–Alfredo De Oro .... Runner-Up–Charles H. Manning
Apr, 1890–Alfredo De Oro .... Runner-Up–Charles H. Manning
May, 1890–Albert G. Powers .... Runner-Up–Alfredo De Oro
Jun, 1890–Charles H. Manning .... Runner-Up–Albert G. Powers
Aug, 1890–Charles H. Manning .... Runner-Up–George N. Kuntzsch
Oct, 1890–Charles H. Manning .... Runner-Up–Albert G. Powers
Jan. 1891–Albert G. Powers .... Runner-Up–Charles H. Manning
Mar, 1891–Albert G. Powers .... Runner-Up–P. H. Walsh
May, 1891–Alfredo De Oro .... Runner-Up–Albert G. Powers
Mar, 1892–Alfredo De Oro .... Runner-Up–Albert G. Powers
Mar, 1893–Alfredo De Oro .... Runner-Up–Frank Sherman
Jun, 1893–Alfredo De Oro .... Runner-Up–P. H. Walsh
Dec, 1895–William Clearwater .... Runner-Up–Alfredo De Oro
Mar, 1896–William Clearwater .... Runner-Up–Jerome Keogh
Apr, 1896–William Clearwater .... Runner-Up–Alfredo De Oro
May, 1896–Alfredo De Oro .... Runner-Up–William Clearwater
Jun, 1896–Alfredo De Oro .... Runner-Up–Grant Eby
Fall, 1896–Herman E. Stewart .... Runner-Up–Alfredo De Oro
May, 1897–Grant Eby .... Runner-Up–Herman E. Stewart

Jun, 1897–Jerome Keogh .... Runner-Up–Grant Eby
Aug, 1897–Jerome Keogh .... Runner-Up–William Clearwater
Mar, 1898–William Clearwater .... Runner-Up–Jerome Keogh
Apr, 1898–Jerome Keogh .... Runner-Up–William Clearwater
Dec, 1898–Alfredo De Oro .... Runner-Up–Grant Eby, Frank Horgan (tie)
Jan, 1899–Alfredo De Oro ....
Apr, 1899–Alfredo De Oro .... Runner-Up–Jerome Keogh
Dec, 1899–Alfredo De Oro .... Runner-Up–Fred Payton
Apr, 1900–Alfredo De Oro .... Runner-Up–Jerome Keogh
Mar, 1901–Frank Sherman .... Runner-Up–Alfredo De Oro
Apr, 1901–Alfredo De Oro .... Runner-Up–Frank Sherman
Mar, 1902–William Clearwater .... Runner-Up–Charles Weston
May, 1902–Grant Eby .... Runner-Up–William Clearwater
Dec, 1902–Grant Eby .... Runner-Up–P. H. Walsh
May, 1903–Title vacant
Nov, 1904–Alfredo De Oro .... Runner-Up–Jerome Keogh
Nov, 1904–Alfredo De Oro .... Runner-Up–Jerome Keogh
Jan, 1905–Alfredo De Oro .... Runner-Up–Grant Eby
Mar, 1905–Jerome Keogh .... Runner-Up–Alfredo De Oro
May, 1905–Alfredo De Oro .... Runner-Up–Jerome Keogh
Oct, 1905–Alfredo De Oro .... Runner-Up–William Clearwater
Dec, 1905–Thomas Hueston .... Runner-up–Alfredo De Oro
Feb, 1906–Thomas Hueston .... Runner-Up–Charles Weston
Apr, 1906–Thomas Hueston .... Runner-Up–Joe W. Carney
May, 1906–John Horgan .... Runner-Up–Thomas Hueston
Oct, 1906–John Horgan .... Runner-Up–Horace B. ("Jess") Lean
Oct, 1906–Jerome Keogh .... Runner-Up–John Horgan
Nov, 1906–Jerome Keogh .... Runner-Up–Fred Tallman
Dec, 1906–Thomas Hueston .... Runner-Up–Jerome Keogh
Feb, 1907–Thomas Hueston .... Runner-Up–Edward Dawson
Apr, 1907–Thomas Hueston .... Runner-Up–Jerome Keogh
Apr, 1907–Thomas Hueston .... Runner-Up–William Clearwater
Jan, 1908–Thomas Hueston .... Runner-Up–Jerome Keogh
Jan, 1908–Title vacant
Apr, 1908–Frank Sherman .... Runner-Up–Charles Weston
May, 1908–Alfredo De Oro .... Runner-Up–Frank Sherman
Oct, 1908–Alfredo De Oro .... Runner-Up–Bennie Allen
Nov, 1908–Thomas Hueston .... Runner-Up–Alfredo De Oro
Apr, 1909–Charles Weston .... Runner-Up–Thomas Hueston
May, 1909–Charles Weston .... Runner-Up–Horace B. ("Jess") Lean
Oct. 1909–John G. Kling .... Runner-Up–Charles Weston
Nov, 1909–Thomas Hueston .... Runner-Up–John G. Kling
Dec, 1909–Thomas Hueston .... Runner-Up–Bennie Allen
Feb, 1910–Jerome Keogh .... Runner-Up–Thomas Hueston
Mar, 1910–Jerome Keogh .... Runner-Up–Charles Weston
Apr, 1910–Jerome Keogh .... Runner-Up–Thomas Safford
Sep, 1910–Jerome Keogh .... Runner-Up–Thomas Hueston
Oct, 1910–Jerome Keogh .... Runner-Up–Bennie Allen
Nov, 1910–Alfredo De Oro .... Runner-Up–Jerome Keogh
Jan, 1911–Alfredo De Oro .... Runner-Up–William Clearwater
Mar, 1911–Alfredo De Oro .... Runner-Up–Thomas Hueston
Apr, 1911–Alfredo De Oro .... Runner-Up–Jerome Keogh
May, 1911–Alfredo De Oro .... Runner-Up–Charles Weston
Nov, 1911–Title vacant
Apr, 1912–Edward Ralph .... Runner-Up–James Maturo
June, 1912–Alfredo De Oro .... Runner-Up–Edward Ralph

Jan, 1913–Alfredo De Oro .... Runner-Up–James Maturo
Feb, 1913–Alfredo De Oro .... Runner-Up–Thomas Hueston
Oct, 1913–Bennie Allen .... Runner-Up–Alfredo De Oro
Dec, 1913–Bennie Allen .... Runner-Up–Charles Watson
Jan, 1914–Bennie Allen .... Runner-Up–James Maturo
Apr, 1914–Bennie Allen .... Runner-Up–Edward Ralph
Jun, 1914–Bennie Allen .... Runner-Up–Ray R. Pratt
Dec, 1914–Bennie Allen .... Runner-Up–James Maturo
Dec, 1915–Title vacant
Mar, 1916–W. Emmett Blankenship .... Runner-Up–Johnny Layton
May, 1916–Johnny Layton .... Runner-Up–W. Emmett Blankenship
Sep, 1916–Frank Taberski .... Runner-Up–Johnny Layton
Oct, 1916–Frank Taberski .... Runner-Up–Ralph Greenleaf
Nov, 1916–Frank Taberski .... Runner-Up–Edward Ralph
Jan, 1917–Frank Taberski .... Runner-Up–James Maturo
Feb, 1917–Frank Taberski .... Runner-Up–Louis Kreuter
Apr, 1917–Frank Taberski .... Runner-Up–Bennie Allen
May, 1917–Frank Taberski .... Runner-Up–Larry Stoutenberg
Oct, 1917–Frank Taberski .... Runner-Up–Joe Concannon
Nov, 1917–Frank Taberski .... Runner-Up–Louis Kreuter
Jan, 1918–Frank Taberski .... Runner-Up–Ralph Greenleaf
Dec, 1919–Title vacant
Dec, 1919–Ralph Greenleaf .... Runner-Up–Bennie Allen
Nov, 1920–Ralph Greenleaf .... Runner-Up–Arthur Woods
Oct, 1921–Ralph Greenleaf .... Runner-Up–Arthur Woods
Dec, 1921–Ralph Greenleaf .... Runner-Up–Arthur Woods
Feb, 1922–Ralph Greenleaf .... Runner-Up–Thomas Hueston
May, 1922–Ralph Greenleaf .... Runner-Up–Walter Franklin
Oct, 1922–Ralph Greenleaf .... Runner-Up–Bennie Allen
Dec, 1922–Ralph Greenleaf .... Runner-Up–Arthur Church
Jan, 1923–Ralph Greenleaf .... Runner-Up–Thomas Hueston
Apr, 1924–Ralph Greenleaf .... Runner-Up–Bennie Allen
Apr, 1925–Frank Taberski .... Runner-Up–Ralph Greenleaf
Apr, 1926–Title vacant
Nov, 1926–Ralph Greenleaf .... Runner-Up–Erwin Rudolph
Jan, 1927–Erwin Rudolph .... Runner-Up–Ralph Greenleaf
Mar, 1927–Erwin Rudolph .... Runner-Up–Harry Oswald
May, 1927–Thomas Hueston .... Runner-Up–Erwin Rudolph
Sep, 1927–Frank Taberski .... Runner-Up–Thomas Hueston
Nov, 1927–Frank Taberski .... Runner-Up–Pasquale Natalie
Jan, 1928–Frank Taberski .... Runner-Up–Arthur Woods
Mar, 1928–Ralph Greenleaf .... Runner-Up–Frank Taberski
May, 1928–Ralph Greenleaf .... Runner-Up–Andrew St. Jean
Dec, 1928–Frank Taberski .... Runner-Up–Ralph Greenleaf
Dec, 1929–Ralph Greenleaf .... Runner-Up–Erwin Rudolph
Dec, 1930–Erwin Rudolph .... Runner-Up–Ralph Greenleaf
Dec, 1931–Ralph Greenleaf .... Runner-Up–George Kelly
Dec, 1932–Ralph Greenleaf .... Runner-Up–Jimmy Caras
May, 1933–Ralph Greenleaf .... Runner-Up–Andrew Ponzi
Dec, 1933–Erwin Rudolph .... Runner-Up–Andrew Ponzi
Feb, 1934–Andrew Ponzi .... Runner-Up–Erwin Rudolph
1934–Title vacant
Dec, 1935–Jimmy Caras .... Runner-Up–Erwin Rudolph
Apr, 1936–Jimmy Caras .... Runner-Up–Erwin Rudolph
Apr, 1937–Ralph Greenleaf .... Runner-Up–Andrew Ponzi
Nov, 1937–Ralph Greenleaf .... Runner-Up–Irving Crane
Dec, 1937–Ralph Greenleaf .... Runner-Up–Irving Crane

BILLIARDS

(140)

Mar, 1938–Jimmy Caras	Runner-Up–Andrew Ponzi
Apr, 1938–Jimmy Caras	Runner-Up–Andrew Ponzi
Apr, 1940–Andrew Ponzi	Runner-Up–Jimmy Caras
May, 1941–Willie Mosconi	Runner-Up–Andrew Ponzi
Nov, 1941–Erwin Rudolph	Runner-Up–Irving Crane
May,1942–Irving Crane	Runner-Up–Erwin Rudolph
Dec, 1942–Willie Mosconi	Runner-Up–Andrew Ponzi
Apr, 1943–Andrew Ponzi	Runner-Up–Willie Mosconi
Dec, 1943–Andrew Ponzi	Runner-Up–Irving Crane
Mar, 1944–Willie Mosconi	Runner-Up–Andrew Ponzi
Feb, 1945–Willie Mosconi	Runner-Up–Ralph Greenleaf
Mar, 1946–Willie Mosconi	Runner-Up–Jimmy Caras
Nov, 1946–Willie Mosconi	Runner-Up–Irving Crane
Dec, 1946–Irving Crane	Runner-Up–Willie Mosconi
May, 1947–Willie Mosconi	Runner-Up–Irving Crane
Nov, 1947–Willie Mosconi	Runner-Up–Jimmy Caras
Mar, 1948–Willie Mosconi	Runner-Up–Andrew Ponzi
Feb, 1949–Jimmy Caras	Runner-Up–Willie Mosconi
Feb, 1950–Willie Mosconi	Runner-Up–Irving Crane
Jan, 1951–Willie Mosconi	Runner-Up–Irving Crane
Feb, 1951–Willie Mosconi	Runner-Up–Irving Crane
Apr, 1952–Willie Mosconi	Runner-Up–Irving Crane
Mar, 1953–Willie Mosconi	Runner-Up–Joe Procita
Mar, 1955–Willie Mosconi	Runner-Up–Joe Procita
Apr, 1955–Irving Crane	Runner-Up–Willie Mosconi
Dec, 1955–Willie Mosconi	Runner-Up–Irving Crane
Feb, 1956–Willie Mosconi	Runner-Up–Jimmy Caras
Mar, 1956–Willie Mosconi	Runner-Up–Jimmy Moore
Apr, 1956–Willie Mosconi	Runner-Up–Irving Crane
Apr, 1963–Luther Lassiter	Runner-Up–Jimmy Moore
Aug, 1963–Luther Lassiter	Runner-Up–Jimmy Moore
Mar, 1964–Luther Lassiter	Runner-Up–Arthur Cranfield
Sep, 1964–Arthur Cranfield	Runner-Up–Luther Lassiter
Mar, 1965–Joe Balsis	Runner-Up–Jimmy Moore
Mar, 1965–Joe Balsis	Runner-Up–Jimmy Moore
Mar, 1966–Luther Lassiter	Runner-Up–Cisero Murphy
Dec, 1966–Luther Lassiter	Runner-Up–Cisero Murphy
Apr, 1967–Luther Lassiter	Runner-Up–Jack Breit
Dec, 1967–Luther Lassiter	Runner-Up–Jack Breit
Apr, 1968–Irving Crane	Runner-Up–Luther Lassiter
Feb, 1969–Ed Kelly	Runner-Up–Cisero Murphy
Feb, 1970–Irving Crane	Runner-Up–Steve Mizerak
Feb, 1971–Ray Martin	Runner-Up–Joe Balsis
Feb, 1972–Irving Crane	Runner-Up–Lou Butera
Feb, 1973–Lou Butera	Runner-Up–Irving Crane
Feb, 1974–Ray Martin	Runner-Up–Allen Hopkins
Aug, 1976–Larry Lisciotti	Runner-Up–Steve Mizerak
Aug, 1977–Allen Hopkins	Runner-Up–Pete Margo
Aug, 1978–Ray Martin	Runner-Up–Allen Hopkins
Aug, 1979–Mike Sigel	Runner-Up–Joe Balsis
Aug, 1980–Nick Varner	Runner-Up–Mike Sigel
Aug, 1981–Mike Sigel	Runner-Up–Nick Varner
Aug, 1982–Steve Mizerak	Runner-Up–Danny DiLiberto
Aug, 1983–Steve Mizerak	Runner-Up–Jimmy Fusco
Aug, 1985–Mike Sigel	Runner-Up–Jim Rempe
Aug, 1986–Nick Varner	Runner-Up–Allen Hopkins
Jan, 1990–Bobby Hunter	Runner-Up–Ray Martin

WOMEN'S POCKET BILLIARD CHAMPIONSHIPS
WORLD 14.1 CHAMPIONSHIPS

Feb, 1974–Meiko Harada .... Runner-Up–Jean Balukas
Aug, 1977–Jean Balukas .... Runner-Up–Gloria Walker
Aug, 1978–Jean Balukas .... Runner-Up–Billie Billing
Dec, 1979–Jean Balukas .... Runner-Up–Mary Kenniston (WPBA Nat'ls)
Aug, 1980–Jean Balukas .... Runner-Up–Billie Billing
Aug, 1981–Loree Jon Ogonowski .... Runner-Up–Vicki Frechen
Aug, 1982–Jean Balukas .... Runner-Up–Jon Ogonowski
Aug, 1983–Jean Balukas .... Runner-Up–Jon Ogonowski
Aug, 1985–Belinda Bearden .... Runner-Up–Mary Kenniston
Aug, 1986–Loree Jon Jones .... Runner-Up–Mary Kenniston

WPBA NATIONAL CHAMPIONS

1978–Jean Balukas .... Runner-Up–Billie Billing (14.1)
1979–Jean Balukas .... Runner-Up–Mary Kenniston (14.1)
1980–Gloria Walker .... Runner-Up–Sabra MacArthur (Nine Ball)
1983–Jean Balukas .... Runner-Up–Belinda Bearden (Nine Ball)
1984–Jean Balukas .... Runner-Up–Mary Kenniston (Nine Ball)
1985–Belinda Bearden .... Runner-Up–Linda Haywood (Nine Ball)
1986–Jean Balukas .... Runner-Up–Mary Kenniston (Nine Ball)
1987–Mary Kenniston .... Runner-Up–Loree Jon Jones (Nine Ball)
1988–Loree Jon Jones .... Runner-Up–Robin Bell (Nine Ball)
1989–Robin Bell .... Runner-Up–Loree Jon Jones (Nine Ball)
1990–Loree Jon Jones .... Runner-Up–Ewa Mataya (Nine Ball)
1991–Ewa Mataya .... Runner-Up–Belinda Bearden (Nine Ball)

WORLD POOL BILLIARD ASSN. WORLD NINE-BALL
CHAMPIONS

Men

1990–Earl Strickland (USA) .... Runner-Up–Jeff Carter (USA)
1991–Earl Strickland (USA) .... Runner-Up–Nick Varner (USA)
1992–Johnny Archer (USA) .... Runner-Up–Bobby Hunter (USA)

Women

1990–Robin Bell (USA) .... Runner-Up–Loree Jon Jones (USA)
1991–Robin Bell (USA) .... Runner-Up–Joann Mason (USA)
1992–Franziska Stark (Germany) .... Runner-Up–Vivian Villareal (USA)

Junior

1992–Hui-Kai Hsia (Taiwan) .... Runner-Up–Michael Coltrain (USA)

PRO TOUR CHAMPIONS—1991–1992

MPBA Sanctioned:

1991 - Rakm-Up Classic - Nick Varner

Seventh Annual Glass City Open - Bobby Hunter

International 9-Ball Classic - Buddy Hall

Dufferin 9-Ball Classic - David Howard

McDermott Masters - Earl Strickland

Sands Nine-Ball Open XIII - Johnny Archer

WPBA Sanctioned:

International 9-Ball Classic - Robin Bell

McDermott Masters - Loree Jon Jones

Sixteenth U.S. Open Nine-Ball - Ewa Mataya

The Big Island Classic - Robin Bell

Wahine Women's Nine-Ball Open - Vivian Villareal

1992 - LA Open - Peg Ledman

International Nine-Ball Classic - Vivian Villareal

McDermott Masters - Robin Bell

Sixteenth U.S. Open Nine-Ball - Buddy Hall
Bicycle Club Invitational - Buddy Hall
Sands Nine-Ball Open XIV - Jim Rempe
1992 - Fifth Rakm-Up Classic - Buddy Hall
Eighth Glass City Open - Mike Lebron
LA Open - Earl Strickland
International Eight-Ball Classic - Efren Reyes
International Nine-Ball Classic - Johnny Archer
McDermott Masters - Earl Strickland
Sands Nine-Ball Open XV - Johnny Archer
Bicycle Club Invitational - Mike Sigel

WORLD THREE-CUSHION CHAMPIONS (PROFESSIONAL)

Year	Champion	Year	Champion
1878	Leon Magnus	1920	John Layton
1899	W. H. Catton	1921	Augie Kieckhefer
1900	Eugene Carter	1921–22	John Layton
1900	Lloyd Jevne	1923	Tiff Denton
1907	Harry P. Cline	1924–25	Robert L. Cannefax
1908	John W. Daly	1926	Otto Reiselt
1908	Thomas Hueston	1927	Augie Kieckhefer
1908	Alfredo De Oro	1927	Otto Reiselt
1909	Alfredo De Oro	1928–30	John Layton
1910	Fred Eames	1931	Arthur Thurnblad
1910	Thomas Hueston	1932	Augie Kieckhefer
1910	Alfredo De Oro	1933	Welker Cochran
1910	John W. Daly	1934	John Layton
1911	Alfredo De Oro	1935	Welker Cochran
1912	Joseph W. Carney	1936	William Hoppe
1912	John Horgan	1936–37	Welker Cochran
1913–14	Alfredo De Oro	1938	Roger Conti
1915	George Moore	1939	Joseph Chamaco
1915	William H. Huey	1940–43	William F. Hoppe
1915	Alfredo De Oro	1944–46	Welker Cochran
1916	Charles Ellis	1947–52	William F. Hoppe
1916	Charles McCourt	1953	Raymond Kilgore
1916	Hugh Heal	1954	Harold Worst
1916	George Moore	1964	Arthur Robin
1917	Charles McCourt	1969	Juan Navarra
1917	Robert L. Cannefax	1972	Juan Navarra
1917	Alfredo De Oro	1984	Ludo Dielis
1918	Augie Kieckhefer	1988	Ludo Dielis
1919	Alfredo de Oro	1989	Torbjorn Blomdahl
1919	Robert L. Cannefax	1990	Raymond Ceulemans

Three-Cushion Records

High Run–Game (50 points) .... Willie Hoppe, 20, 1928
High Run–Match (360 & 1,000 points) .... Willie Hoppe, 15, 1936–50
High Average–Game (50 points) Sang Lee, 3.125, 1992 Otto Reiselt, 3.125, 1926
High Grand Average–Match (1,400 points) .... Willie Hoppe, 1.18, 1947
High Grand Average–Tournament .... Willie Hoppe, 1.33, 1950

WORLD THREE-CUSHION CHAMPIONS (AMATEUR)

1928–29 ..... Edmond Soussa, Egypt
1930 .... H. J. Robyns, Holland
1931 .... Enrique Miro, Spain
1932–33 ...... H. J. Robyns, Holland
1934 .... Claudio Pugvert, Spain
1935 .... Alfredo Lagache, France
1936 .... Edward L. Lee, U.S.A.
1937 .... Alfredo Lagache, France
1938 ..... Augusto Vergez, Argentina
1948 .... Rene Vingerhoedt, Belgium
1952 .... Pedro L. Carrera, Argentina
1953 & 58 .... Enrique Navarra,
Argentina
1960 .... Rene Vingerhoedt, Belgium

1961 .... Adolfo Suarez, Peru
1963–73 ...... Raymond Ceulemans,
Belgium
1974 ..... Nobuaki Kobayashi, Japan
1975–80 ...... Raymond Ceulemans,
Belgium
1981 .... Ludo Dielis, Belgium
1982 ...... Rini Van Bracht, Holland
1983 . Raymond Ceulemans, Belgium
1984 ..... Nabuaki Kobayashi, Japan
1985 . Raymond Ceulemans, Belgium
1986 .... Avelino Rico, Spain
1987 .... Torbjorn Blomdahl, Sweden

Three-Cushion Records

High Run (U.S.A.)–Game (50 points) .... Bill Hawkins, 19, 1977
High Run–Game (60 points) .... Marcello Lopez, 15, 1964
.... R. Ceulemans, 15, 1975
.... A. Gonzales, 15, 1979
High Average–Game (60 points) .... R. Ceulemans, 2.5, 1966
High Grand Average–Tournament .... R. Ceulemans, 1.679, 1978

BILLIARDS

144